Kissing
Bill O'Reilly,
Roasting
Miss Piggy

Kissing Bill O'Reilly, Roasting Miss Piggy

100 Things to Love and Hate About TV

Ken Tucker

St. Martin's Press
New York

www.stmartins.com

Library of Congress Cataloging-in-Publication Data

Tucker, Ken, 1953–
    Kissing Bill O'Reilly, roasting Miss Piggy : 100 things to love and hate about TV / Ken Tucker.—1st U.S. ed.
        p. cm.
    ISBN 0-312-33057-X
    EAN 978-0312-33057-6
    1. Television—United States. I. Title.

PN1992.3.U5T76 2005
791.45'0973—dc22   2004051443

First Edition: February 2005

10 9 8 7 6 5 4 3 2 1

To my mother,

Ann Tucker (1927–2004),

who taught me to read anything and everything,

and to watch TV with pleasure and skepticism

Contents

Acknowledgments   xiii
Introduction   xv

Love: Edie Falco   1
Hate: David E. Kelley   3

Love: Jennifer Garner's wig   6
Hate: *Star Trek*   8

Love: Ricky Nelson   9
Hate: *Seinfeld* theme music   11

Love: David Caruso   13
Hate: Ed Asner/*Lou Grant*   15

Love: MTV's *Real World*   17
Hate: MTV's music videos   19

Love: *NewsRadio*   22
Hate: *The Kids in the Hall*   24

Love: *Cops*   26
Hate: Bald/Macho: *Kojak* and *The Shield*   27

Contents

Love: *Full House*/T.G.I.F. shows   31
Hate: *The Brady Bunch*   35

Love: C-SPAN   38
Hate: Sunday morning news shows   40

Love: Aaron Spelling shows   42
Hate: Reality TV   44

Love: Abbott & Costello   47
Hate: *Rowan & Martin's Laugh-In*   48

Love: Andy Rooney   52
Hate: Viewers for Quality Television   54

Love: James Garner   57
Hate: Paris Hilton and *The Simple Life*   60

Love: *Homicide: Life on the Street*   62
Hate: William and Robert Conrad   64

Love: *Buffalo Bill*   66
Hate: *M*A*S*H*   68

Love: Bill O'Reilly   71
Hate: Geraldo Rivera   73

Love: Michael Mann's cop-show trilogy   75
Hate: Made-for-TV movies   77

Love: Marg Helgenberger   81
Hate: John Larroquette   83

Love: *MacGyver*   85
Hate: Home makeover shows   87

Love: Simon Cowell   90
Hate: *American Idol*   91

Love: Best mothers   95
Hate: Worst mothers   100

Love: Best fathers   107
Hate: Worst fathers   112

Love: *Andy Griffith Show/The Honeymooners*   118
Hate: *Barney Miller*   119

Love: David Duchovny   122
Hate: *Six Feet Under*   124

Love: *Freaks & Geeks*   127
Hate: *The Price Is Right*   129

Love: Informercials   131
Hate: *The Tonight Show*   133

Love: *Roseanne*   139
Hate: The Smothers Brothers   141

Love: David Brinkley   144
Hate: Edward R. Murrow   145

Love: Alec Baldwin in *Knots Landing*   148
Hate: Vincent D'Onofrio on *Law & Order: Criminal Intent*   150

Love: *The Joy of Painting*   153
Hate: Michael O'Donoghue & *SNL*   156

Love: Jack Benny   158
Hate: The "Golden Age" of Drama   160

Love: *Ramona*   164
Hate: TV animals   166

Love: *The Point*   169
Hate: *A Charlie Brown Christmas*   170

Love: *Profit* and *Vengeance Unlimited*   173
Hate: Bochco and the "story arc"   176

Love: Richard Hatch   179
Hate: *Queer Eye/As Folk*   181

Love: Johnny Rotten on *American Bandstand*/Tom Snyder   184
Hate: Howard Stern on TV   185

Love: Homer Simpson   188
Hate: *Mystery Science Theater/The Family Guy*   190

Love: Pee-Wee Herman   193
Hate: The FCC   195

Love: *Silk Stalkings*   198
Hate: *West Wing*   200

Love: Paul Lynde   203
Hate: Miss Piggy   205

Love: *Pardon the Interruption*   207
Hate: PBS   208

Love: Lisa Bonet on *The Cosby Show*   212
Hate: "Tackling" Issues   213

Love: William H. Macy on *SportsNight*   216
Hate: The women of *Law & Order*   217

Love: *Laverne & Shirley*   221
Hate: *Whoopi*   223

Love: The Best *Twilight Zones*   226
Hate: The Worst *Twilight Zones*   227

Love: *Twin Peaks*   229
Hate: Final episodes   231

Love: *Welcome Back, Kotter*   235
Hate: Chuck Barris   236

Contents

Love: *The Waltons*   240
Hate: *Little House on the Prairie*   243

Love: *Batman*   245
Hate: Nostalgia   248

Love: Pamela Anderson's breasts   251
Hate: Sex on TV   252

Acknowledgments

Thanks to the editors of *Entertainment Weekly*, Jeff Jarvis, Jim Seymore, and Rick Tetzeli, for giving me the opportunity to look at so much TV and get paid for it; to the Museum of Television and Radio in New York, for many hours of viewing pleasure and pain; to my wily, riotous agent, John Campbell; to my wise, wry editor, Diane Reverand, and her shrewd, adroit assistant, Regina Scarpa; to my exemplars in criticism, Robert Christgau, John Leonard, Wilfrid Sheed, and Sanford Schwartz. And all love to Anne, who inspires me beyond writing.

Introduction

A fluid, of-the-moment, democratic, "cool" medium, television is wickedly difficult to pin down in prose—it inherently resists final judgments, tidy arguments, and any history that won't be outdated three seasons after Heather Locklear adds another TV series to her resume.

As a consequence, most of the writing that's been done about it comprises a strangling accretion of false pieties and half-recalled history. Misplaced nostalgia has grown up around it: the prose equivalent of slowly choking vines.

This is utterly at odds with the burning bush of television itself, which warms us and gets us all het up, which generates constant, passionate feelings of devotion, betrayal, loyalty, and mistrust that give the lie to passive cliches like "vegging out in front of the boob tube."

In my experience—my own, my family's, my friends', my observation of strangers'—everyone has a firm belief in what he or she loves and hates about TV, whether this belief system is formed while watching that episode of *Seinfeld* in syndication for the twenty-ninth time, or waiting to see which sad young thing some pathetic bachelor/ette will choose.

This book is written in the spirit of television itself. It's about moments, scenes, genres; it's about an actor's gesture or the shape of her sentences; it's about an entire series' run or a personality that broke through a show to reach into us. The entries are arrayed as randomly as the way a viewer switches from channel to channel. I play favorites—I'm not going to hide the fact that I'm a baby boomer who has contempt for the Gen X and Y know-nothingism that passes for a lot of TV criticism these days. But I'm also not going to deny that I've gotten as much cultural sustenance from *Buffy the Vampire Slayer* as I have from the novels of Philip Roth.

Which is not to say that I think *Buffy* is as essential to the culture as the best of Roth. One thing this project has reaffirmed to me is the transitory value of TV versus the wisdom to be gleaned from more formal works of art—art that TV at its most clever parodies, alludes to, and aspires to. But when a character in one of the shows I love said, "Reared by TV—imagine that," I laughed and felt like crying. Too many of us *are* reared by TV, to our detriment; all the more reason to make discriminations, to resist the temptation to say, "I love TV" or "I hate TV"—it's more complicated than that.

Those complications inspired this book. I've chosen the 100 number, split 50/50, because it's convenient, sure, and because I like the way lists can cohere as an argument—in this case, that TV not only amuses, hypnotizes, or bores us, but that it gets at deeper issues in the culture, provoking discussions that no longer reach millions of people via books or movies.

In placing these love/hate entries alongside each other, I hope they sort of talk to each other as well as to you, sparking connections between sitcoms, commercials, the news, and *The Simpsons* in ways they would not otherwise. Please: read, watch, agree, argue.

Kissing
Bill O'Reilly,
Roasting
Miss Piggy

Love

The Greatest Soprano: Edie Falco and Carmela's Manicure

In a series marinated in the Mob machismo of its male stars—and has there ever been a male star more imposing than James Gandolfini's bear-with-the-heart-of-a-snarling-puppy-dog Tony Soprano?—*The Sopranos*'s most complex, emotionally nuanced character is its female lead, Edie Falco as Tony's wife. In the pilot, Carmela is adither about a party she's throwing; she acts as though she prefers to remain as ignorant as possible about the details of her husband's occupation as long as the cash enables her to keep their Jersey mini-mansion spiffy and her manicure gleaming. What could have been an ambivalent, even weak role became, via Falco's sad, tragic glances and fleeting but volcanic temper flare-ups, a crucial alternative to the series' men-screw-up-and-screw-over/women-fuck-or-die ethos.

Who knows whether creator David Chase planned it this way or began to see it as the cameras rolled, but Carmela quickly transcended the laquered-hair crime-family harridan enshrined in Martin Scorcese films. By *The Sopranos*'s fifth episode, "College," Falco had a poignant subplot in which she invites the family priest—Father Phil, a smarmy moocher—over for dinner and a movie. Carmela's loneliness often manifests itself as a desire for compliments and to learn more about culture (two areas in which her husband is woefully wanting), and so she was easy prey for Father Phil's raves for her cooking and his half-baked auteurist theories. They came close to kissing—a triple Catholic sin, I would calculate—but Carm came to her senses. Toward the end of that first season, she observed the cleric exhibiting similarly creepy behavior on others, and righteously tells him that he exploits "spiritually thirsty women."

On her career report card, you might say that Falco plays well with boys: A few appearances on the grungy *Homicide: Life on the Street* cemented a friendship with producer-writer Tom Fontana, who took her to HBO and a recurring role in his male-dominated-to-put-it-mildly prison series *Oz*. Director-writer Hal Hartley used her in two of his male-menopausal films, and John Sayles, one of the movies' strongest writers for women, wrote her a role in his 2002 *Sunshine State*. An experienced stage actress, she has appeared in off-Broadway and Broadway productions including *Side Man, Frankie and Johnny in the Claire de Lune*, and *Shooting Gallery*.

But Falco will always be best known for *The Sopranos*. Carmela only grew more central to the show as her marriage grew weaker and her two children entered noxious adolescences. Tensions peaked at the end of the fourth season, when Carmela and Tony had a rattle-the-plaster argument that pushed both actors to their finest, most subtle yet explosive performances to that date. By the fifth season, Tony and Carmela have separated, and she roams the house as though it's an abandoned castle, forced to be both nuturer and protector, resenting both roles. A sucker for love and book-learnin', she entered into a queasy relationship with her son's guidance counsellor (David Strathairn), as written, a far too hasty, hard-to-believe attraction, but once again, Falco redeems the writers' material for the way she quickly scribbles down the teacher's book recommendation—Flaubert's *Madame Bovary*, of which she's clearly never heard—on a scrap of paper, promising, "I'll stop by Borders on the way home and get it." And says it in such a way that you know that, unlike her mob-wife friends, she'll also *read* it.

Hate

The Most Overrated Writer in Prime-Time History: David E. Kelley

A boomer Boston lawyer who used his law degree in court for three years and in the TV industry ever since, David E. Kelley is the ambulance chaser of the airwaves. He's never met a cultural hotpoint he hasn't tried to haul into a script to make a quick buck. You name it, he's perverted it: Capital punishment, pro- and con-; religious beliefs versus hard-headed science; teachers having sex with students on *Boston Public*; corpulent people ridiculed (a recurring theme in all his shows); *Ally McBeal*'s Fish (Greg Germann) jonesing for the neck wattles of Judge Jennifer Cone (Dyan Cannon); Randy Quaid, on *The Brotherhood of Poland, NH*, putting a crimp in his married-sex life because he has a "Katie Couric fetish"; and the Fonz's fetish exposed: Henry Winkler, playing a dentist on *The Practice*, likes to watch women in spike heels squish cockroaches.

Kelley is the *L.A. Law* producer who sent semiregular tough-"bitch" attorney Rosalind Shays (Diana Muldaur) spiralling down an elevator shaft to boost the series' sagging ratings and get the star characters making "splat" jokes well into the next season. He's the guy who invented the bucolic, Mayberry-like town of *Picket Fences* and then populated it with verging-on-the-perv characters like a guy who broke into people's homes only to take baths. He had Mandy

Patinkin bite off the tip of a costar's finger in *Chicago Hope* to settle an argument. All right, that last one doesn't sound too out of character for anyone who's seen the frequently over-the-top Patinkin in concert—I think Patinkin would probably do that if his piano player plinked a bum note. All of Kelley's shows seem to start off with the crisp, well-ordered intelligence of an impeccably composed legal brief but sooner or later devolve into a succession of cheap stunts and surreal running gags, like *Ally McBeal*'s dancing baby (a water-cooler topic for a day; a tiny big bore for subsequent months).

Known for his old-school work ethic, famous for writing entire seasons of shows in longhand on yellow legal pads, Kelley is a control-freak freak. I was once told by a writer who's since gone on to create shows for NBC and HBO that the year he spent on the staff of *Picket Fences* was "the most boring period of my life—you'd write a scene based on Kelley's story idea, and then he'd take it away and rewrite it completely. Or he'd just cut you out completely—you learned nothing. Having a writing staff was a needless expense for the network." Kelley hit a career high point during the 1999–2000 season when he managed to wedge five shows onto the air: *Chicago Hope* on CBS, *The Practice* and *Snoops* on ABC, and *Ally McBeal* and *Ally* (a curious half-hour version that edited the series as pure sitcom) on Fox. During this period he became the first producer to win Emmys for best drama (*The Practice*) and best comedy (*Ally McBeal*) at the same ceremony.

Beloved in Hollywood, an industry town where an East Coast pedigree and a star wife (Michele Pfeiffer) excuses a lot of self-indulgence as long as the latter is productive labor that snags media attention, Kelley is the most overrated, highly decorated scribe in Los Angeles. His feature films *Mystery, Alaska* (1999), *Lake Placid*

(1999), and *To Gillian on Her 37th Birthday* (1996) have been squishy flops, and 1999's *Snoops*, girl-girl private eyes complete with "nipple cams" for surveillance work, and 2002's *Girls Club* (girl-girl-girl lawyers) reiterated his career-long obsession with squabbling, preferably catfighting women. These shows disappeared after a mere few episodes.

Don't get me wrong: TV could use its own prime-time Marquis DeSade, a producer-writer who'd really get into the muck of human (and sometimes animal) sexuality. But Kelley is such a company-town man that his thematic quirks never lead to any interesting or revelatory point. They're just gimmicks, gussied up with well-structured plots and snappy dialogue. He gets good performances out of actors early on in his shows' runs—think Kathy Baker in *Fences* or Peter McNichol as a pesty lawyer in *Chicago Hope*. In the initial editions of *McBeal,* Calista Flockhart was an adroit ditz, not the cartoon she later was forced to become. He even knows how to switch professions and doctor an ailing show, allowing Robert Downey, Jr., to bring welcome earnestness and wit to *McBeal* and letting James Spader deploy his arsenal of smooth-smuggie mannerisms to great effect in the cast-decimated 2003 season of *The Practice*.

But sooner or later, Kelley always succumbs to the cute, the cutesy bizarre, the coyly controversial. He's like so many of his characters: a master of the fascinating come-on, he never goes all the way.

Love

Jennifer Garner's Red Wig

The image that stuck in everyone's head after they saw the pilot of *Alias* was the hair that was stuck *on* Jennifer Garner's head: a flaming-red 'do that resonated with anyone who'd seen the movie *Run Lola Run,* and anyone else who had a pulse. Series creator J. J. Abrams is a young master at making comic-book imagery take on flesh-and-blood substance; at combining superheroics with soul-rattling emotion; of treating the TV screen as though it was a movie screen, filling it with color and action and the sound of clever chatter. The scenes we all loved in the pilot were the moments just after Garner's Sydney Bristow, a CIA double agent, has mourned the murder of her fiancé. Abrams makes sure every sight, every sound, every gesture has a motive—it's what distinguishes him from an entire generation of young filmmakers who are big on visuals and short on storytelling skills. In this case, he has Sydney—now on the run from the baddies but also, simultaneously, running straight toward them to seek revenge—dyes her hair red to throw off her pursuers. It's a trick. Who'd seek out an exhibitionist, who swivels her pert bottom through a crowded airport, drawing stares for the way her crimson tresses waggle to the rhythm of her hips?

If the script says dye job, we know from seeing Garner in natural-brown-hair repose that this was a wig, and all the more blazingly erotic later on, when, shackled to a chair, tortured (pliers, teeth, blood), she and her hair flip themselves over in an impossibly thrilling move to land squarely on top of her torturer, turning the tables—er, chairs. It's what made *Alias* the most galvanizing new show of 2001.

Abrams had been deeply involved with hair before *Alias*. As one of the creators of *Felicity*, he'd had to take some responsibility for the fact that when actress Keri Russell cut off her Titian curly locks, ratings dipped alarmingly. Hair may even have been on his mind when he cooked up the show that would make Jennifer Garner (a fleeting bit player on *Felicity*) a star: "One day I was in the *Felicity* writers' room," he told me. "And I said, sort of as a joke, 'The greatest thing would be if Felicity was recruited by the CIA, because then she could be going on these secret missions, living this life that she couldn't tell [her boyfriends] Ben or Noel about, dismantling bombs.' Of course that couldn't happen in *Felicity,* but it could be another show."

The daydream became *Alias*. "I had a lot of concerns about the tone of the show," Abrams says. "For it to work in a world of *Charlie's Angels* and *Austin Powers,* if the show was satire it would lower the stakes considerably. I also didn't want the show to be so self-serious that it became like you were laughing at it." He achieved it: no camp, real emotions. Well, *some* camp—once they heard and felt the response they got to the red wig, Abrams and his writers proceeded to use the spy excuse to put Garner in a weekly S&M fantasy outfit: rubber minidresses, too-small maid's uniforms, and what seemed like a different hair color every week, including shamrock green.

It's the red one that got things going, though. It symbolized both the passion and the fun that *Alias* was going to be. You could say that a series that came a season later, *24,* must have been inspired by *Alias*—after all, *24* also features dense huggermugger plots, and its central figure, Kiefer Sutherland's Jack Bauer, spends a lot of time,

like Garner's Sydney, bound and shackled. No one ever wants to see
Kiefer Sutherland in a red wig—that's a one-way ticket to Bozoville.
But *everybody* wants to see Sydney Bristow in a red wig.

Hate

Star Trek Sucks

It always sucked. In any of its various incarnations. NBC was right
when, in 1969, after three seasons and poor ratings, it cancelled
Gene Roddenberry's mush-brained, wooden-dialogued, sub–Rod
Serling–style sci-fi parable for intergalactic equal rights and the inspiration for millions of idiot cultists wearing pointy "Spock" ears at
comic-book conventions and in movie-theater lines. Damn syndication afterlife reruns! Pop culture never needed William Shatner, and
it especially didn't need the "knowing," self-parodying Shatner he's
become. All the spin-offs of *Star Trek* suck, too. Even Patrick Stewart, a decent but stiff and inexcusably peevish actor, who should get
down on his knees and thank the God Show Business every day that
he was cast in one of these career cash cows, because otherwise no
one would be casting him in *X-Men* and his *Christmas Carol* one-
man shows wouldn't be packin' 'em in. Really, if you want science
fiction, read Tom Disch or Philip K. Dick. The last time I watched
an entire episode of *Star Trek* was when I was in high school and
Paula, a girl I had a crush on, liked to get stoned and watch Shatner-
and-Nimoy-era *Trek* reruns. I thought it sucked even while I was
stoned; my only other coherent thought was that Paula had beautiful hands.

Love

Ricky Nelson Subverts Himself in
The Adventures of Ozzie and Harriet in 1964

Ricky Nelson married Kris Harmon in 1963. In keeping with the semirealism for which his father, Ozzie, the series' onscreen chuckling, doofy dad, former jazz bandleader and also the behind-the-scenes shrewdie producer-director, strove, Kris was immediately integrated into the series, just as older brother David's wife had been dragged onscreen a few years earlier. Everyone in the Nelson family not only earned a paycheck, they earned their SAG card.

Most of the time, *Ozzie and Harriet* (1952–1966) was as harmless and comfortable as a vintage *Archie* comic book, complete with "gee whiz!" exclamations from the boys, and a parade of Bettys and Veronicas slinking through episodes as the guys' malt-shop dates— yes, there was a permanent malt-shop set, built primarily to score easy food jokes off of the series' own Jughead, Rick's roly-poly best buddy, Wally, played by the delightfully weird, giggly Skip Young.

Things changed somewhat in the late '50s, when the real-life Ricky fell under the spell of Sun Records, New Orleans R&B, and Elvis Presley in particular. If Elvis was the Hillbilly Cat, Ricky was the Hollywood Kitten—he even hired Presley's guitarist, James Burton, to back him. Rick parlayed his rosebud-red lower lip, his vacant erotic gaze, and pleasantly flat voice into a hit single in '57—a cover of Fats Domino's "I'm Walkin'." Ozzie, not so much of a jazz snob that he didn't recognize a good commercial thing, tacked a Ricky performance onto the end of an episode that aired that year having nothing to do with the plot. In essence, Ozzie Nelson helped invent the music video.

In the deceptively ordinary 1964 episode entitled "Kris Plays Cupid," Kris and her friend, Ginger (Charlene Salerno) plot to provoke Wally into proposing to Ginger. We get a wonderfully kitschy look at Ricky and Kristin's home: They eat dinner watching TV like zombies, seated at chairs into which are built trays to hold plates, like grown-up school desks. There's a lot of foolishness as Kristin and Ginger conspire to lure Wally into Ginger's grasp, this despite the fact that Wally has found a new blonde to date. The episode ends with another comic-book echo. Commenting blandly on Wally's actions, Ricky says to Kristin, "You know the old saying, variety is the spice of life," at which point Wifey actually *picks up a frying pan and chases him out the door.*

The story is over, but wait: Ricky, dressed in a suit and tie, his familiar guitar with his name embossed on its body, has appeared with his three-piece band to sing a song. It's business as usual, until you start listening to the lyric Nelson sings. A self-penned ditty called "A Happy Guy," it's a concise but rockin' little number in which Ricky disavows a 9-to-5 job and a white-picket-fence life, pronounces his disdain for wearing a businessman's suit and tie, and announces his true desire: "to pick up and go / Where the four winds blow," and that's why (and here he rounds his way into the choral title phrase), he's a happy guy.

In other words, Ricky is telling us he'd rather be doing precisely the opposite of what's shown on *The Adventures of Ozzie and Harriet*—teasing his female fans with the fantasy of being foot-loose and single, and expressing those yearnings on a show under his father's watch. By 1964, Ricky's hits had begun to fade—that year, only one of his songs, "For You," went Top Ten. He wouldn't have another hit until 1972, after he'd changed his name to "Rick" and recorded "Garden Party." Five years after that, he'd divorced Kris, citing her alcohol and drug problems, and had become an inveterate touring musician—the very guy who liked "to pick up and go where the four winds blow" sung about in "Happy Guy."

On that 1964 *Ozzie and Harriet* episode, Ricky was giving the game away, singing from his heart in a way that contradicted everything else he was doing professionally. Did the home audience dig the disparity then? If they were adults, they may have been too busy tuning out, or if they were teens too busy grooving on the music. ("A Happy Guy" is a terrific, buried-treasure single.) In any case, the adventures that Ricky Nelson was taking in his mind were bursting the bonds of *The Adventures of Ozzie and Harriet*.

Hate

The Worst Theme Music of All Time: *Seinfeld*

Hey, love *Seinfeld*, 99.9 percent of it. Can watch it in reruns just about any evening and get some chuckles: Jason Alexander had some brilliant seasons, Julia Louis-Dreyfuss did some inspired, underrated slapstick, Michael Richards did too much, overrated amount of the same. Jerry is indomitable: the Robocop of stand-up comedy, unstoppable, utterly awe-inspiring in his unslakable thirst for getting the next laugh, on nightclub stage or on small screen.

And there have been, God knows, thousands of examples of awful theme music. Not even counting the schlock shows, *The Brady Bunch* theme is of a piece with the rest of that show's puerility; the *Gilligan's Island* theme, which of course restates the moron-simple plot of the show in awkward couplets, isn't even amusing as camp. Both sets of lyrics were written, by the way, by the shows' creator, Sherwood Schwartz. As far as instrumental themes go, the worst prolific composer has got to be Mike Post, purveyor of lousy pseudo-jazz-rock from *The Rockford Files* to *Hill Street Blues* to *Law & Order*.

But the worst theme music for a classic television series must be Jonathan Wolff's work on *Seinfeld*. That awful, lurching tempo; that shameless funk finger-plucking bass guitar line; that woozy, self-consciously "zany" melody—it goes against everything Jerry Seinfeld stands for, which is clean, crisp, clear entertainment. The music didn't just stink up the opening and closing credits, of course—it was played under the stand-up routines Jerry did at the beginning and the end of the early seasons, and during scene transitions—always distracting, always so Hollywood, so un–New Yorky for this most New Yorkish of shows. It's one thing for Wolff to have brought such a meretricious style to the *Arsenio Hall* talk show during Wolff's stint as grinning-boy bandleader; it's fine for him to junk up junky shows from *Who's the Boss?* to *Good Morning, Miami*. But, *man*—listening to that Seinfeld anti-jazz-funk just gets more stomach-churning as each syndication year passes.

Love

David Caruso Pins a Hood to the Wall: A Star Is Born

In the pilot of *NYPD Blue* (1993), most of the focus was on Dennis Franz, a veteran of *NYPD* exec producer Steven Bochco's *Hill Street Blues,* who had also taken his character into Bochco's short-lived *Beverly Hills Buntz.* Now he was Det. Andy Sipowicz: a good cop gone boozer, bending rules till they snapped back right between his bloodshot eyes. The true auteur of *NYPD* was writer David Milch, himself a reformed alky, who put a lot of emotion into the decline, fall, and redemption of Sipowicz. As good as Franz was—and he was frickin' great, ready to be as truculently sour and unsympathetic as Milch wanted him to be, recognizing the role of a lifetime: Archie Bunker with a badge and moral rot—what no one counted on was the fact that the show would also skyrocket the good fortune of its costar, David Caruso.

Caruso was a young actor whose red hair, pug nose, and pale skin had kept him in the background—colorfully, but in the background—of episodic TV like Michael Mann's *Crime Story* (see Mann entry), in which he had a minor role. But as Det. John Kelly, all quiet power and grace, grateful for Sipowicz's mentorship and determined to see his partner regain control of his life, Caruso suddenly commanded the camera. He used an old, cheap actor's trick—declining to make eye contact with anyone lest he appear engaged by anything other than his own Zen-like soulsearching meditations—to steal a lotta scenes.

The best of these occurred three-fourths of the way through the pilot, when, with Sipowicz in the hospital, gunned down by a mobster, Caruso's Kelly invades a Manhattan crime boss's lair and sits down opposite the kingpin to demand the whereabouts of the boss's offending employee. When a flunky leans over to muscle Kelly out of the room, Caruso rises like the wrath of God and just grasps the creep's throat and slams him up against the wall, never taking his eyes off the crime boss. As the strangling hood gasps, Caruso's Kelly says to the boss, "Tell Giardella that John Kelly wants to see him." To punctuate the sentence, he gives the punk another solid slam against the wall—you can see plaster break and fall.

It's the moment Caruso became a star to millions. Soon enough, his ego would puff, he'd get standoffish with his costars—even Franz, an apparent prince of a fellow about whom you can never find an unkind word. Bochco himself once told me that the "only bigger prick I ever worked with than Caruso was Daniel Benzali"—the cueball-skulled star of the producer's *Murder One,* who also happens to be in this *NYPD* pilot as a gleaming defense lawyer. Caruso would leave *NYPD* after this first season, mistakenly smelling success as a feature-film career. As of this writing, a humbler version of Caruso is refraining from making eye contact on *CSI: Miami.* Plaster no longer crumbles; the element of menace that complicated his heroism has been drained off. Still, too many scripts revolve around his *CSI* character, forensic investigator Horatio Crane, vowing to solve a crime for a suddenly orphaned child or widowed wife—it's hard to believe the actor doesn't push this flagrant savior-complex into the plots. Sometimes it seems as though Caruso is pinning himself to a wall, his own hand wrapped around his own throat, threatening to take the wind out of another vibrant, breathing character.

Hate

Lou Grant Knows Better Than You

The series called *Lou Grant,* in which Ed Asner took his patented gruff-but-lovable *Mary Tyler Moore Show* character and moved him from sitcom TV-station producer to drama-show newspaper editor, was excessively praised at the time of its premiere in 1977, mostly because cocreator James L. Brooks was such an intelligent fellow. In addition to *MTM,* he would go on to oversee *Taxi* a year later, have the taste to extract *The Simpsons* from *The Tracy Ullman Show,* and, in feature films, write and direct *Broadcast News* (1987), one of the best romantic comedy-dramas ever set in the media world.

But *Lou Grant,* which took place at a paper called the *Los Angeles Tribune*—a sort of cross between the *Los Angeles Times* and, given Nancy Marchand's Katherine Graham–like turn as publisher, *The Washington Post.* In other words, Lou was no longer an underdog as he'd been at *MTM's* WJM. He was a big-dog overlord surrounded by eager pups—Robert Walden's scrappy Joe Rossi and Linda Kelsey's spaniel-eyed Billie Newman—anxious to do some scooping to impress the boss. The underlying theme that Brooks would address with a sure, light touch in *Broadcast News*—the commodification and superficializing of the news—was dealt with on *Lou Grant* with a much heavier hand. Grant and Marchand's Mrs. Pynchon usually acted as though the fate of journalism rested on the way they guided their paper's coverage of topics like pollution, Vietnam-veteran rights, and neo-Nazi hate groups. As the critic John Leonard has written, this was "a series that worried more about the ethics of news gathering than most journalism schools." A show like this could only be diminished by including comic relief, but sought it anyway, in the person of Animal, played by Daryl Anderson, a dippy, post-hippie photographer.

The ponderousness of *Lou Grant,* which increased as the show went on over the course of five droning seasons, cast a retrospective pall over the fine comedic acting Asner had done on *MTM.* I remember watching *Lou Grant* at the time and thinking, This is where the initial meeting between Lou and Mary, the famous "You've got spunk . . . I *hate* spunk!" scene, is revealed for how it would have played out in a more real life: "You've got spunk . . . and I'm *threatened* by spunk! *I'm* the only one who gets to embody spunk! Get outta my office!"

In life, Asner's increasing interest in world politics—in particular, his objection to American involvement in Central America—hastened the cancellation of *Lou Grant.* With the peculiar myopia endemic to TV criticism, most reviewers on the television beat cited Asner's politics as a probable cause for *Lou Grant's* demise but were more upset that the series didn't have a chance to give its fans a fond "farewell episode" wrap-up rather than exploring the ease with which both the network and the public accepted the fact that one man's politics could make a show disappear faster than a Sandinista dissident. That said, I don't think America lost much with the whisking-away of *Lou Grant* in 1982. And as the years go by, it becomes easier to forget the logy debates and urgent-issues-tackled that clogged the airwaves, and easier to remember a time when Ed Asner was better than a glib poster-boy for liberal pieties—when he was a deft comic actor sparring, with Tracy-Hepburn ease, with Mary Tyler Moore.

Love

MTV and *The Real World*

Most pundits saw MTV's gradual move into game shows and "reality" shows as a betrayal of its original mission, which was . . . *what,* exactly? To spread lousy surrealisms and narcissistic rock-band commercials-for-themselves throughout the nation? Thank God for *Singled Out,* the 1995 dating show that gave us Jenny McCarthy, initially hired as a standard-issue blonde-babe announcer but whose raucous, slap-their-asses-right-back interactions with the rabid male contestants in the audience made the show fun. MTV did less innovation in the music world—unless you count a competition to give away John Mellencamp's pink house as a breakthrough in promoting a singer's hit-single-of-same-name a breakthrough—until it got into more traditional programming. Only when the channel started casting about for ways to boost its ratings and took a chance on dicey prospects like the minimally produced, maximally attituded cartoons *Beavis & Butt-Head* and *Daria,* or the gross-out stunts on *The Tom Green Show* and Johnny Knoxville's *Jackass,* did MTV truly acquire an identity as something more than record-company shill. Few remember that Jon Stewart got his talk-show start on MTV, or that Adam Sandler was, right from the start, an inscrutable yet goofball-funny guy who was—well, not even a cohost but more like a daily hanger-on—on the 1980s' *Remote Control.* True, for every Stewart there's been a blight like Dan Cortese, the MTV sports nut who somehow finagled a career in bad sitcoms (*Veronica's Closet*; a '90s remake of *Route 66* [Dan, I saw George Maharis, and you, sir, are no George Maharis—or even Martin Milner]; and *Rock Me Baby*), and Tabitha Soren, the MTV News correspondent who was as much of a reporter as Butt-Head.

You could say that *Total Request Live,* hosted most popularly by ex-divinity-student Carson Daly, was little more than an updated *American Bandstand.* In fact, Daly said it all the time, Dick Clark being an idol whose wisdom he sought out while doing the show. But Daly, unlike Clark, actually telegraphed his opinion about the music he was playing, through inflection, wink, or outright disgust. At its late-'90s height, you couldn't beat this afterschool phenomenon (*TRL,* not Daly himself) for its screaming-fan energy.

Best-known of all, *The Real World,* the prototype of the modern "reality-TV" genre was conceived by producers Mary-Ellis Bunim (who died in 2003) and Jonathan Murray. As always in this genre, reality is manipulated—young contestants chosen in part for their potential to clash are plunked into dream houses in cities that ranged from San Francisco to Paris. Fueled by the close quarters, liquor, and ever-increasing self-awareness that the way to make a media splash via this show was to be a pain in the ass, *Real World* contestants acted out. The wacky, crude bike messenger Puck (in 'Frisco) and the *Real World: New York*'s sullen Kevin Powell (who went on to a career as a writer of perfectly dreadful poetry), as well as such famous-among-fans moments as the slap Stephen gave Irene in *Real World: Seattle*— all of this amounted to a revitalization not of "reality" but of soap opera for the MTV generation. In its latter-day existence, *The Real World* has become thirty minutes of booze-fueled come-ons ending in lurching group-gropes. This increasingly disgusting spectacle culminated, during the taping of *Real World: San Diego,* with the alleged rape of a friend of one of the "cast members" by a crew member in a bathroom where no camera was present.

Still, for as long as *The Real World* was novel, more innocent, and a tad more sober, it was fun. The same can be said of every aspect of MTV, with the necessary addendum that nothing on the channel— which repeats its successes and failures over and over and over to fill out its twenty-four-hour programming day—stays novel for very long.

Hate

MTV and the Invasion of the Music Video

When it was launched in 1981, MTV was essentially what its letters stood for: "music television," a nonstop array of very specifically "rock" songs (not R&B, not country), illustrated via filmed or taped mini-movies, introduced by "veejays." "Music television" was thus actually "visual radio." Like the radio of that era, it had rigidly formatted playlists and mostly mediocre announcers. Where radio demanded nice voices, TV demanded telegenic personalities. Except for the quick savviness and lugubrious tones of Kurt Loder, the channel never produced any intriguing star of its own, but rather a succession of familiar faces, starting with blandly "nice" personalities such as Martha Quinn, so perky she qualified for anti-pimple-cream commercials endorsements, and annoyingly "cool" personalities as the cooing pseudo-Goth, Nina Blackwood. Bob Pittman, the smooth-talking, former-radio-exec huckster who likes to take credit for creating MTV, has been frequently quoted as describing the channel as "a pure environment" and MTV, or the channel itself as "the program"—that is, one seamless stream of entertainment and advertising. Music videos were, in a sense, nothing new. At least as far back as the '20s, animated cartoons were scored to jazz compositions by the likes of Louis Armstrong and Duke Ellington. Richard Lester was making music videos within a feature-film framework in *A Hard Day's Night* and *Help!* The Beatles' own *Yellow Submarine* was an extended cartoon video. Queen took Fritz Lang's *Metropolis,* applied bombast and Freddie Mercury's screech to its soundtrack, and turned it into a looooong music video. These were discrete entities. MTV presented music video as a genre of programming, one that quickly fell into a rut of clichés. There was the male rock band lip-synching while either writhing women or "surreal" (incongruous or abstract) images floated around or behind the musicians. There were the videos that "told stories." Michael Jackson, in part as a way to become the first MTV-era black musician to break the channel's white-rock color barrier, was a proponent of narrative videos gussied up as mini-movies, such as the feeble John Landis–directed horror spoof built around the song "Thriller."

Even the most clever music videos were boring by the second time you saw them. They tended to literalize lyrics that once yielded richer, multiple associations when a song just floated from the radio into your mind. It frequently became impossible to separate a song from its video representation. Who can think of Eurythmics' "Sweet Dreams" without picturing those stupid cows lowing in a field? By new millennium, we had Sisqo's "The Thong Song" (sole motif: thonged women jiggling) and now music was being created precisely *to become bad videos.*

There are no winners in music video. When Bruce Springsteen

decided to avoid the cult of personality by declining to appear at all in a video he made for his song "Atlantic City," he filled the allotted time it took to play the song with grainy images of barren New Jersey landscapes that inevitably left one thinking about Springsteen's visual inspirations (Walker Evans?) rather than the song itself. Music videos date a song much more quickly than the music itself does. They are tedious commercials for creations that ought to be experienced without the mediation of filmic technique, let alone an intro by a toothy veejay. Music videos are evilly banal.

Love

NewsRadio: WKRP as a Comedy

The late-'90s sitcom about a New York City all-news radio station was a classic "workplace comedy" that's never really received its proper due. As created by writer-producer Paul Simms, who'd also worked on *The Larry Sanders Show, NewsRadio* provided most immediately an opportunity to see that star Dave Foley could do a lot more than the self-indulgent, adolescent Monty Pythonisms of his *Kids in the Hall* period in Canada. Foley, playing the WNYX news director, has a quality that distinguished him from other comic actors. He knows how to portray a shy, polite, introverted man who is not a total dweeb. Phil Hartman, as the show's co-anchor, did a brilliant job in a difficult role: How does anyone do a boob anchorman without aping the definitive one, Ted Knight's Ted Baxter? Hartman figured out how to do it. His Bill McNeal isn't a simple fool—he's a mean fool, someone who relishes making other people squirm. It's a testament to Hartman's stylized but genuine charm—with his crinkly eyes and lizard's smile—that he makes Bill as likable as he is. The other major force in *NewsRadio* is the station's owner, Jimmy James (Stephen Root), a squinty-eyed shrewd businessman with a whiff of a Southern accent. There's a black-humored edge to Jimmy. When asked what he was going to do after work one day, he responded, "I don't know; maybe I'll go downstairs and find a bar fight." Root, his perpetual scowl echoed by the false jollity of his tone, could take an odd line for a sitcom joke, like, "There's enough bad vibes in this room to run a hoodoo factory," and make it simultaneously funny and the musing of a man who believes that hoodoo will catch up to him some day.

If Foley, Hartman, and Root were the series' most prominent players—rarely has office politics, the incessant struggle for leverage, power, an office sofa, and a bigger salary been portrayed with more subtlety than in this seemingly conventional sitcom—*NewsRadio* had a prodigious backbench—that is, aside from Joe (*Fear Factor*) Rogan, who played the series' amiable handyman, a role that had originally been held by then-barely-known comic Ray Romano, who lasted, by his telling, exactly one day on the set. Hartman's co-anchor, Catherine Duke, was played with serene reserve by Khandi Alexander, who went on to give a blazing-eyed, furiously passionate performance in HBO's magnificent inner-city miniseries *The Corner*. It was as though Alexander was letting off steam from *NewsRadio*; as good as the series was, it was clear the writers had no idea how to write for a brainy black character and make her as funny as the rest. She then opted to pick up a well-deserved network paycheck as a coroner with the annoying tic of talking to corpses in *CSI:Miami*.

Maura Tierney became a regular on *ER*, managing to make exhaustion, alcoholism, and loneliness both poignant and sexy at a time when that long-running series was running out of interesting characters. Andy Dick became, for a time, a public joke (out of control from substance abuse) before hitching up with another sitcom, *Less Than Perfect*, that underuses his oddball skills—the jittery neurotic, Don Knotts as a mean little schizo.

Hartman was murdered in 1998. The show had to write in his character's death, and he was replaced by an awkward Jon Lovitz for another, far weaker, season. *NewsRadio* never got the respect it merited from its network, but you should seek it out in syndication for its delicately turned acting and its still-cutting humor. In the sub-genre of media-world comedies, it's no *Mary Tyler Moore Show,* but it sure as hell holds up better than *Murphy Brown.*

Hate

The Kids in the Hall: Canadian *Merde*

Saturday Night Live producer Lorne Michaels continued his unbro-ken record of never having produced another good TV show since *SNL* with this discovery from his native Canada. Five comics—Dave Foley, Scott Thompson, Mark McKinney, Kevin McDonald, and Bruce McCulloch—had teamed up to do a frosty version of the *Monty Python* troupe, right down to a fondness for absurdist humor and dressing in drag. *Monty Python's Flying Circus's* taped segments were accompanied by tempered tittering on the soundtrack, but *The Kids in the Hall,* which launched as an HBO special in 1988 and then became a regular series airing on HBO, the CBC in Canada, and—briefly, bowdlerized—on CBS, was accompanied by a grat-ingly loud, hooting laugh track to goose the Kids' exceedingly mild, audaciously derivative humor. Half-*Python,* half-*SNL, The Kids* de-veloped a cast of such semiregular oddball characters as McKinney's shrieky, beak-nosed, webfooted, white fright-wigged "half-human chicken lady" and the fellow commonly referred to as "the head crusher," who peered at people in the distance and imagined that he was squashing their heads between his fingers. Like *Python,* the Kids would occasionally step out of a sketch to comment on it. Fans view this as daringly postmodern; the rest of us shrug at the easy-way-out, seen-it-before tedium that characterizes *Kids*.

A typical *Kids* sketch consisted of a long, drawn-out pseudo-biography of the recently deceased, fictional Cyril St. John, "the great vaudeville entertainer." There are interviews with people who knew him, who recount his famous, early 1930s stunt "The Escape from the Large Wet Paper Bag." The joke is that St. John never escaped from the straitjacket in which he'd been trussed. As the decades wore on, he starred in a sitcom called *Fit to be Tied* and movies such as *Bound to Serve*. (Are you laughing yet?) The voiceover narration pokes you in the ribs until they're broken: "While commonly considered his greatest film," the narrator intones, "it was also considered to be bad."

These one-joke ideas, presented over and over, were typical of the Kids' style, which attracted a fervent cult following—*cult* being the significant word—and the group disbanded in 1995. Some of these talented men, like Foley on *NewsRadio* and Thompson on *The Larry Sanders Show,* went on to better projects that validated their comic worth.

Love

Cops

There's a sense in which I find *Cops* one of the most consistently pleasurable, soothing series I've ever seen. I know that, had there not been *Cops* camera crews around, the police officers shown from Broward County, Florida, to Portland, Oregon, would probably not be quite so civil and by-the-book as they are to the suspects they either interrupt or intercept while on their daily patrols. I know there would probably be a lot more cursing, more bending of civil rights, more cynical judgments made against the people under suspicion or caught in their various illegal acts. Yet I'm sure its millions of viewers feel the same way I do since the series premiered in 1989: safe, assured, lulled into the belief that, if anyone were to try to break into my house, the cops would come lickety-split and arrest the bad guys.

At the same time, *Cops* is a tremendously valuable social document. Its roving documentary vignettes have created one of the few sites at which America can view the lives of poor people—people against whom crimes are committed far more often than to me and probably you, people whose dire circumstances compel them to commit those crimes. *Cops* dwells most often on the fringes of society and yet reminds us that the fringe is part of the fabric of our country and that fringe takes in a lot of territory, comprising a lot of lives. The great documentary filmmaker Frederick Wiseman has made massively long, heartbreaking movies about the sort of people

Cops lets us merely glimpse in each of its brief half hours—what the ruling media, the upper-middle-class, and the rich consider marginal folks, "bad" people. Wiseman and the producers of *Cops* know that there's an alternative America that is never reflected on the network and cable news, in sitcoms, in dramas, in "reality TV."

Sure, there are many times when *Cops* seems to exploit its subjects. The more hard-hearted among you may say a criminal gets what he or she deserves, including the indignity of being pushed to the pavement and handcuffed roughly. The joke about *Cops*—and it's been made very wittily and with appropriate bleakness in the marvelously poker-faced, similarly politicked Comedy Central series *Reno 911!*—is that its cameras love nothing more than a fat, naked victim or perpetrator to boost the titillation-and-pixilation factor, to keep viewers amused or shocked.

The irresistible allure of *Cops* to me—and perhaps to you, too?—is that I know that, but for the grace of Something Or Other, I could easily be a poor devil with his teeth feeling the tension between the street cement and the boot, or be the wearer of the boot, testing a terrible power.

Hate

Baldness as Macho: Kojak and *The Shield*'s Vic Mackey

In sitcoms, bald guys are either stuffy figures of ridicule like *The Dick Van Dyke Show*'s Mel Cooley (Richard Deacon, an intemperate stuffed shirt who deserved a film director like Preston Sturges to give him some sharp elbow room) or salt-of-the-earth cranks like *Every-*

body Loves Raymond's Frank Barone (Peter Boyle, who used the menace of his youth in films like *Joe* to mellow into sitcom misanthropy). So why, when they star in dramas, do baldies turn into walking phallic symbols, either pulsing with cocky confidence or throbbing with anger? Telly Savalas's hairless Theo Kojak became so well known for his tiresome catchphrase—"Who loves ya, baby?"—and the lollypop lolling around in his motormouth (a phallic symbol within a phallic symbol!) that it's easy to forget that Kojak started out a pretty cool customer. TV and movie veterans Abby Mann (writer) and Joseph Sargent (director) made a tough, laconic, 1973 fact-based TV-movie, *The Marcus-Nelson Murders,* that introduced the character. The one-shot flick got such big ratings and positive reviews that CBS quickly put Savalas—until that point typecast as a menacing supporting actor in movies like *The Dirty Dozen*—on retainer as the star of a weekly series.

The concept became a hit but lost its grit. Savalas savored not only the lollypops his character chewed to avoid smoking but also the limelight. He turned the character into a parody of macho excess, not just on *Kojak* itself but in variety-show guest appearances in which he hammily spoofed himself. Fingering his character's snap-brim hat, he even cut cocktail-music albums, as though "Who loves ya, baby?" was the stuff of Frank Sinatra standards. Kojak became, in short, a pain in the ass but unavoidable—a lump in the pocket of pop culture. If there had been Viagra in the '70s, you can bet Savalas would have shilled for it.

Contrast this to Michael Chiklis's chrome-dome police detective Vic Mackey, who was an asshole right from the start of *The Shield,* which premiered in 2002. Conceived as a series that would establish the amorphous FX network as a cutting-edge, no-holds-barred, it's-not-HBO-it's-basic-cable young-male-demo-grabber, *The Shield* presented itself as the real deal in cop shows. Never mind that NYPD blue language: Steven Bochco's officers were still heroes. On *The Shield,* the hero broke the law! Why, in the premiere, he even killed a guy who was going to rat him out! And never mind that premium-cable raunch—Mackey had a posse of yahoo cops who partied hard with babes and drugs!

Chiklis, who'd started off his career by taking a role no name actor wanted—playing John Belushi in an adaptation of Bob Woodward's anti-Beloosh book *Wired*—had climbed back to respectability and a decent livelihood in the mediocre, standard police series, playing a teddy-bear cop in *The Commish* (1991–1995). By the new millennium, he was up for inflating his show-biz image; he needed a breakthrough role. He found it in creator Shane Ryan's self-conscious, shaky-handheld-camera outlaw-cop show; Chiklis shaved off the last few strands on his skull and bulled his way through L.A. squad rooms, crack dens, and Mackey's own terrified family home.

For his strenuous overacting, Chiklis was rewarded with an Emmy in *The Shield*'s first season. The show succeeded in giving FX a clear identity. The network followed it with another laboriously self-conscious rule-breaker, this one about the world of cosmetic surgery, *Nip/Tuck*. Chiklis, however, must have felt a film of flop sweat forming on his naked brow, because in just its second season, *The Shield* was already looking tired—Mackey's bullet-headed bluster was already looking like a Kojak. By season three, the series closed out with its lowest-rated finale yet, even as the writers tried to work up sympathy for its antihero with a subplot about his child's autism. Nope; that was just shameless, not character-building. Vic Mackey is a dick and *The Shield* thinks it's ballsy; both exist in a wet dream.

Love

***Full House* and the Auteurs of "TGIF"**

From the late '80s through the '90s, parents parked their kids in front of a slate of sitcoms that offered an implicit guarantee that there wouldn't be any "edgy" hanky-panky or violence onscreen for at least two hours every Friday on ABC. I know, I know, all you '80s nostalgists reading this: The shows to which I refer above never actually existed simultaneously as a two-hour block on ABC's "Thank Goodness It's Friday" lineup of family-oriented sitcoms. The lineup shifted and swerved over the years (anyone recall something entitled *Just the Ten of Us?*), but the essential, most likable TGIF show was *Full House,* which premiered in 1987. The show that unleashed Ashley and Mary-Kate Olsen upon the world in the form of a single, adorable tot, Michelle, was your basic sitcom built around a stand-up comic, Bob Saget, who played your basic widowed single dad, Danny Tanner. Danny had both help and hindrance raising Michelle and her older sisters D. J. (Candace Cameron) and Stephanie (Jodie Sweetin) from his wannabe-rock-star brother-in-law, Jesse (John Stamos), and his kooky best friend, Joey (Dave Coulier).

As created by Jeff Franklin and produced by Thomas L. Miller and Robert L. Boyett, *Full House* was schlock, but surprisingly rich, loamy schlock that really explored what an unconventional family unit could be, without being self-conscious or self-important about it. Saget was able to turn his nightclub-comic persona (a downright filthy-joke comedian with an impish grin) into an acceptable TV image and overcome the paycheck job of hosting the appalling *America's Funniest Home Videos* while making amusingly muttered, ad-libbed-sounding remarks that proved he was aware of the commercial enterprise he'd signed on for. He wasn't too proud or pretentious to give it his all when called upon to be a caring, loving father.

For TV siblings, D. J., Stephanie, and Michelle were very different personalities who didn't fall into the usual sitcom rut of merely hating each other. They squabbled and competed for Dad's attention, but they also established healthy relationships with the two other men in their lives. Stamos, who in real life was just enough of a rock musician to sub occasionally as a Beach Boy in that group's Brian Wilson–less endless-tour phase, managed to convey Jesse's ambition and lecherousness without having those qualities spill over into his exchanges with the kids, while Coulier, a genuinely gifted impersonator, raised the bar for doofus best friends.

A show like *Full House* can become popular and run for years just repeating its formula into exhaustion, but as this one proceeded, it even managed to introduce a good new character—Lori Loughlin's beguiling Rebecca. She was hot enough to snare Jesse for good and sweet enough to charm the Tanner girls and the kids at home. The series also mined comic gold from a stock character, The Boy-Crazy Dork, in this case D. J.'s deliriously gabby friend Kimmy Gibbler (Andrea Barber, where are you now?).

Miller and Boyett became the auteurs of the TGIF set. They also launched, in '89, *Family Matters,* a spin-off from an earlier Miller-Boyett TGIF show, and certainly the pair's funniest if among their less popular, *Perfect Strangers.* I'll shorthand that show for you: stage-savvy stars Mark Linn-Baker and Bronson Pinchot tried to leverage themselves to bigger things à la Tom Hanks and Peter Scolari's *Bosom Buddies*. They were funny, they lasted seven seasons, but they never had the kid-magic or adult-word-of-mouth appeal that would have given *Strangers* a firmer place in the TGIF fundament.

Family Matters started with the minor *Strangers* character of an elevator operator, Harriette Winslow, played by Jo Marie Payton. Her husband was Carl, the portly but deft Reginald VelJohnson—from his girth to his name, he recalled a black Jackie Gleason (remember the Great One's alter ego Reginald Van Gleason?), and in a better world, VelJohnson would have been nearly as popular. They had three kids, plus Harriet's sister Rachel (Telma Hopkins from—oh, pop-culture overload!—*Bosom Buddies*).

But the show got hijacked by a bit player, an annoying twerp named Steve Urkel, portrayed by Jaleel White in thick glasses, where's-the-flood? trousers, and a whine that could make distant dogs howl. Urkel was something new: a black nerd. This was nothing less than a TV version of progressivism, since Urkel wasn't a stooge or an emasculated young male, but just the opposite—a bookworm who wanted to worm his way into the heart of the Winslows' daughter Laura (Kellie Shanygne Williams).

The other notable Miller-Boyett/TGIF show was *Step By Step,* in which *Three's Company*'s Suzanne Somers and *Dallas*'s Patrick Duffy found a new audience as second-marrieds-with-children. Critics, when they deigned to notice the show at all, branded it a *Brady Bunch* rip-off, but *Step* was more interesting for the way the writers were encouraged to make it clear that Somers's and Duffy's characters had that newly hitched, hot-for-each-other aura, and the six kids from this "blended" family rarely made the gesture toward becoming reconciled to each other. While never degenerating to the creepy vulgarity of Fox's *Married . . . with Children, Step By Step* also avoided the waxy sentimentality of the Bradys.

But, but, you ask: How do I reconcile my hatred of *The Brady Bunch* elsewhere in this book with my fondness for the TGIF shows, which are of barely superior quality? Simple: None of these shows made more than a light dent in the culture (okay, there were a few years there when Steve Urkel's tagline, "Did I do that?" was annoying, but this was balanced by the marvelous campiness of Urkel-Os, an actual cereal product on supermarket shelves), whereas *The Brady Bunch* distorted minds forever with the notion that trash and nostalgia are good; indeed, that *anything* is good if it remains lodged in your mind beyond your high-school years.

Although ABC didn't drop its "TGIF" designation officially until 2000, the programming strategy as a miniphenomenon ended long before that—I'd date it to the moment Jaleel White, by the late '90s too old for the part and anxious to try something else, did his own version of Jerry Lewis's *The Nutty Professor* and took on a sleazeball-romancer alter ego, Urkel's cousin Stefan (pronounced, in what I like to think was a shameless sop to those wacky French critics who adore Lewis, "Stef-AHHNN"). I don't have much use for the TV-fan term "jump the shark," but Urkel-emulating-Jerry was definitely the moment when kids of all ages decided: Thank God Friday's over.

Hate

The Brady Bunch: So Dumb It's . . . Bad

There is no television series I loathe more than *The Brady Bunch*. It is loathsome on a number of levels, much like the stacked boxes upon which the show's nauseatingly winsome stars appear in the opening credits. *The Brady Bunch* is not merely bad—its badness is self-evident: the wooden acting by all of its stars, especially the six child stars' encouraged amateurishness and Robert Reed's ill-disguised I-should-be-doing-Shakespeare boredom. This is combined with scripts that feature laff-lines like, "Vampires can be a pain in the neck!" Indeed, the very fact that *The Brady Bunch* is "bad TV" (corny, artificial even by the standards of its early-'70s sitcom artificiality) is what people use as an excuse for their fondness for it. This is the I-know-it's-junk-but-I-grew-up-in-front-of-it argument, as though nostalgia trumps the will to resist insidious insipidity.

To be sure, badness is what has given *The Brady Bunch* its camp cachet—its enduring life as a totem of guilty-pleasure TV, as well as its postproduction cottage industry of TV-movie reunions, cast-member memoirs, and spoof feature-film adaptations. If you combine its badness and its camp/guilty-pleasure with its day-glo philistinism, this 1969–1974 series inflates to the level of hatefulness.

Take a look at just one well-known episode—and actually, via syndication and long Gen-X memories, *every* episode of *The Brady Bunch* is well known. It's what the invaluably canonical cable channel TV Land meticulously refers to as "episode 80." Dad Reed, mom (Florence Henderson) and the rest of the brood are dragooned by eldest daugher Marcia (Maureen McCormick) into performing for a school talent show fundraiser. Forget—just try—the early minutes in which Mom attempts to extract herself from the task, only to have Dad deliver the line, "If your mother wants to chicken out, it's her chicken," to laugh-track guffaws so loud you may be confused for a second into thinking the words make comedic sense.

Consider the main subplot, in which Dad decides he and eldest boy Greg (Barry Williams) should recite a Henry Wadsworth Longfellow poem, "The Day Is Done." Upon first beginning to intone its singsong rhymes, the three boys enact exaggerated boredom. Big fake yawns and snoring sounds signal to viewers not only that they think the poem is boring (tee-hee), but that *poetry itself is intrinsically boring*. By now, this is so common a belief among Americans that it barely registers as the crass philistinism it is. At the time, this ostensibly wholesome sitcom fare—creator Sherwood Schwartz's fantasy of a second-marriage "blended family" before that term was coined—was sending out a fairly new message in a series that strove to insert an instructive and uplifting message into every wretchedly produced episode. It was—I must use the word again—a *bad* message, a cynical one that has reverberated through the decades on television: that high art is dull, that education is a drag, that there is (to be specific) no difference between a mediocre poet like Longfellow and a great one like Wordsworth or, God and Sherwood Schwartz forbid, Wallace Stevens.

Dad and Greg decide they must enliven their recitation of Longfellow by making it *entertaining,* and so in its high-school performance, whenever Dad or Greg drone the words "mist" or "rain," the other two sons offstage douse them with water. Similar taking-the-words-literally yuks provide this show's antic climax. Creator

Schwartz may as well have had monkeys (or Monkees) performing this humor.

On its surface, *The Brady Bunch* is harmless crud, and even I would forklift *Brady* mom Florence Henderson from the *Brady* pit of aesthetic hell, but only because she has proven to be such a pleasant surprise, a smart, nice person on talk shows. On the other hand, I'd push Barry Williams even farther down to a more grotesque ring of Dante's inferno for his ceaseless-unto-middle-age exploitation of his brief stardom by producing smutty autobiography and smirking cameos wherever he can secure some TV face time. If you dig beneath its crud-crust, *The Brady Bunch* reveals a pernicious form of rot that has created its own aesthetic. This is the aesthetic of the So Dumb It's Good, a position so moronic/ironic as to be unassailable by sensible people seeking to make distinctions between the good and the good-bad.

It's an aesthetic that helped create the culture of semiliterate trivia cultists who go to conventions and onto the Internet to gabble about their favorite moments of *Brady* banality. It is an aesthetic of idiot provincialism that has made television a more stupid, joyless environment. Fuck you, *Brady Bunch*.

Love

Brian Lamb and C-SPAN

Is there a more lovable man on television than the determinedly unlovable Brian Lamb? For maintaining an unreadable poker face while grilling government officials and authors, he is one of the only true exemplars of objective journalism in television history. Hell, for inventing the concept of C-SPAN in 1979 (C-SPAN2, its even more bookish spin-off, lit up in 1986), an all-news, no star-reporters, no montage-editing, let-the-camera-stay-in-one-place-and-roll phenomenon, Lamb deserves the Pulitzer, the Polk, the freakin' Nobel, as far as I'm concerned. C-SPAN is the only network that, every election year, covers the Libertarian Party's convention in its entirety. C-SPAN is the only place to go to watch gavel-to-gavel Congressional hearings. C-SPAN is as likely to cover a speech by Noam Chomsky as it is a conference at the Cato Institute.

Lamb's Indiana-bred plainspokenness is nowhere more in evidence when he talks about ratings, as he did in an interview with the Web site reason.com. He claimed that ratings services hurt C-SPAN's coverage: "There are several things that the press demands you be involved with in order to cover you in any extensive way. One is personality. Two: ratings. Three: profit. And four: advertising. If you don't move money to somebody's bottom line, or if you don't move money in the stock market, or if you don't look and walk and talk like a business, the press automatically loses interest."

Lamb refuses to succumb to the cult of personality; it's said that he's never uttered his own name on the air. In itself, this is not a great virtue, but it's certainly different—like so much of the C-SPAN concept—and simple, and admirable in that simplicity: Lamb creates an identity for his network by creating a cult of no-personality. He told another interviewer, "I don't care that you notice that I'm there, but I don't want you to keep saying to yourself, 'Why won't he get out of my way?' "

The way Lamb declines to become involved in the natural attention-getting or star-making process of television almost amounts to a fetish. For instance, all those books his C-SPAN2 channel *Booknotes* covers via author interviews? Lamb claims that "a book is chosen *before* it's read, not after it's read. A book is chosen because it's a hardback, it's nonfiction, and the author has never appeared on *Booknotes* before. Nor will they appear again under our ten-and-a-half-year tradition. It's a one-shot deal."

A public affairs network that provides in-depth coverage of national and international issues. That's as likely to have a gasbag like Christopher Hitchens taking questions from a citizen in Topeka as it is to let an eloquent historian like Richard Norton Smith take us on a tour of Franklin D. Roosevelt's home and gravesite. It's the only place to go when you want to see those daily White House press conferences or those frequently raucous National Press Club dinner speeches. To be terribly irreverent for a moment, I paraphrase from the King James version of *The Book of Common Prayer* and praise that Lamb of cable, who takest away the sins of television. Have mercy upon him, and sing praises unto his name.

Hate

Sunday Morning News Shows: Hacks, Equivocators, Bloviators, and Twerps with Bow Ties

NBC's *Meet the Press*, which premiered in 1947, and CBS's *Face the Nation*, beginning in 1954, are among the oldest shows on television, "public affairs programming," they used to call it, featuring just what they do now: interviews with news and policy makers on Sunday mornings. Late to this frequently drowsy nonparty is ABC's *This Week with David Brinkley*, which debuted in 1981, when Brinkley was sixty-one years old. All three shows are shellacked with a surface coating of sobersidedness, beneath which lies the flimsy fiberboard of flattery-to-power, to get the big guests on TV, especially the president's men (no matter who the president is at the time, and his "men" *are* usually men), a reflexively secretive, often arrogant bunch who need to be coddled while making it look to the viewer as though tough questions are being asked. The trick is to lob puffball inquiries across the table in the manner of inquiring about grave matters of state.

If this was a conventional history book, I'd run through the various *Meet* and *Face* hosts, but most people nowadays don't know their Laurence Spivak from their Martin Agronsky. If one cast of characters stands out, it's the crew poor Brinkley had to suffer, consisting of George Will, the conservative bow-tie twerp with a baseball-geek habit to try and make himself seem normal, Cokie Roberts, the former NPR hard-news reporter gone warm and soft, and Sam Donaldson, the bad-toupee loudmouth best known, in "reporter" mode, for bellowing questions at various presidents. (A cynosure of TV news is that aggressive volume of questioning, a falsehood Donaldson proved every time he opened his mealy mouth.) Brinkley—who gets closer attention in the news-anchor entry in this book—was the only Sunday morning host to ask flinty follow-up questions, but the format of working with the other three chuckleheads eventually drowned him out and wore him down. He retired in 1996 and was replaced by a non-bow-tie-wearing twerp, former Bill Clinton aide George Stephanopoulis, who tried to boost his third-place show's ratings by featuring a new set that looked like it was pieced together from the William Shatner *Star Trek* flight deck. Stephanopoulis is such a TV newbie that he can't even fake asking tough questions—he exposes the Sunday talk shows for the shams they are.

Meet the Press's Tim Russert, who took over in 1992, is just the opposite: so Boston-Catholic-working-class-tough, he makes a barked "Good morning!" sound like an accusation unto the Lord. But he, too, collapses in the face of the ruling administration. Heavy on his homework, he can rattle off both up-to-the-minute and arcane stats he knows his interviewees can't possibly be prepared to know, yet lets officials off the hook as soon as he establishes that his notes are better than their selective memories. He sets up an unfair and spurious fight, but never gets into the kind of hard-nosed follow-up-and-argue debates his show exists to stage. It's called *Meet the Press*, Tim, not *Press the Flesh*. Same goes for the rest of you guys and gals, may you rest in peace. And, dead and living, I know that you do. Which annoys the hell out of me.

Love

The Most Underrated Producer in TV History: Aaron Spelling

No, I'm not gong to tell you that *The Love Boat, Fantasy Island, Beverly Hills 90210*, or *Dynasty* were great TV series—I don't go in for the camp school of TV drool. And yes, I didn't include *Melrose Place* on that list intentionally, because it was *good*. Spelling is a great executive producer in the sense that he can hand over control to a good producer-writer when he feels he or she knows how to do the job. Brenda Hampton's corny but sweet-hearted *7th Heaven* is a good example. He also takes chances few other moguls in his cushy position would bother trying. That's as true of the gently modulated late-'70s drama *Family* (Sada Thompson and a young Meredith Baxter-Birney in the closest TV will come to Updike/Cheever country) as it is of a stylishly frenetic flop like the Dennis Farina detective series *Buddy Faro* (1998).

Spelling gave Michael Mann, then a fledgling TV writer, a chance to create *Vega$*. Mann subsequently left the Robert Urich sleuth show after its first season, frustrated that he couldn't explore the darker themes he wanted to pursue. Mann wouldn't have gone on to cocreate *Miami Vice*'s Crockett and Tubbs had he not done time writing for Spelling's *Starsky & Hutch*. I like the idea that Spelling, the man whom the Internet Movie Database lists as possessing the "largest single-family home in the state of California," is a smiley little gnome with a soft voice and an iron fist. He'll take a flyer on an excitingly garish piece of Southern Gothic like *Savannah*

(1996) and give the old heave-ho to a petulant Shannon Doherty when her off-camera behavior threatened the value of real estate like *90210*.

Spelling exec-produced the 2003 drug-lord miniseries *Kingpin* at a time when its violence and ethnicity made it less than a long shot on network televsion, just as, at the start of his producing career, he oversaw 1965's *Honey West*, starring Anne Francis as the sexiest detective TV would allow on the air. The man who gave us both *The Mod Squad* and *Charlie's Angels* can never be accused of failing to exploit both counter- and pop-cultural trends, yet he always found time in his business dealings to manufacture interestingly offbeat fare like *The Guns of Will Sonnett* (1967), a kind of TV version of *The Searchers* in which Walter Brennan and then-hottie Dack Rambo, as Brennan's grandson, combed the Old West for Dack's father, a legendarily elusive gunfighter.

Okay, so even if Spelling hadn't green-lit *B.A.D. Cats* in 1980, it's likely that star Michelle Pfeiffer would have gone on to better things . . . but maybe she wouldn't have scampered so fast? Spelling, who started his career as an actor, appearing in episodes of the '50s *Dragnet* and credited as "Gas Station Man" in a '55 edition of *I Love Lucy,* remains a nonstar who enjoys making stars of others. This is as true as helping to invent one—like Farrah Fawcett in *Angels*—as it is in sustaining careers, as he did for his friends Robert Wagner and Stephanie Powers in *Hart to Hart* (1979–1984). If that means he also turns out a TV-movie like *Satan's School for Girls* (1973), where's the harm, ultimately? If for no other reason than he shepherded *Family,* executive-produced Robert Altman's terrific 1974 gambling feature *California Split,* and practically created Heather Locklear (*Dynasty, T. J. Hooker, Melrose*), the guy deserves an Emmy taller than he is. Which may only be a couple of inches bigger than regulation size.

Hate

The Glacial Pace of Reality TV

The end of the '90s and the beginning of the twenty-first century saw the rise of "reality television," from amusing democracy mockeries like *Survivor* (hey, everybody gets a vote, right?) to (no-)talent competitions like *American Idol*, from elaborate dating games like *Temptation Island* and *The Bachelor* to endurance tests of social behavior like *Big Brother*. Oh, and crap like *Fear Factor*, in which people *eat* crap for money. Most of these shows are not so much the horrible affronts to civilization their critics tut-tut them as being, but they are sad, tawdry time wasters.

Reality TV is here to stay as a genre, taking its place alongside sitcoms and dramas. Only a fool would believe they'll burn out and fade away. People want to watch this stuff or it would disappear, pronto. What I wonder, however, is how long the public is going to put up with the ungodly long time it takes to resolve most of these series, which stretch out their climaxes over too many hours, whether it's the crowning of the American Idol or the revelation of a newly radiant Swan.

We're told that young audiences have the attention spans of cheese-distracted rats, that they have no patience for the storytelling of conventional hour-long dramas or become impatient if the jokes in a sitcom don't come with BB-gun rapidity. So why do people watch weeks upon weeks of the audition process of *American Idol,* when by now even the most ardent fan must know that the producers stuff the show with clunkers and ringers who are there just to be insulted and laughed off? Okay, it was mildly amusing the first time, but the twentieth? Why do people watch the designated bachelor or bachelorette so gradually winnow down the possible soul mate, sitting through padded-out editing that replay the same social gaffes, the same spatty fights, over and over?

I believe it's because the attention-span theory is wrong. The young demo the networks so much want to reach adjust their interest level according to the format they're watching. Reality TV is actually a form of soap opera—the old-fashioned, glacially paced afternoon soap, the sorts of shows in which you can miss five episodes and still catch up pretty quickly on what everyone has been up to. Me, I still seem to agree with the majority of Americans who continue to watch the few conventionally structured, so-called "scripted" series—i.e., works of imagination by actual writers—that invariably top the Nielsen ratings. As I write, these are shows such as *CSI* and *Without A Trace.*

Just as soap opera fans tend to gravitate toward one show they follow faithfully, most reality devotees fixate on one or two series that suit their predilections. For this reason, I have preferred *The Amazing Race,* in which contestants scurry around the world in pairs, competing against other pairs to reach a final gold-at-the-end-of-the-foreign-land destination, because I hate to travel and like to watch others go through the hell of it for me. At the other extreme, I like *Big Brother,* in which a group of people are locked inside a rather small, minimally furnished house with no contact with the outside world and have to interact socially just well enough to survive but just cannily enough to get other people voted out and re-main the last inhabitant, because my dream in life is never to have to go outside, to have an unseen network crew bring in food and clean-ing supplies, to spend days just pondering a spot on the wall while deflecting banal chitchat from foolish faux-friends in whom I have no emotional investment.

Does this make me an odd duck? No more so than the millions of viewers who get off on the eating-scorpions-mashed-in-a-blender stunts on *Fear Factor* or who become emotionally invested in the body-toned, inarticulate lugs of failed reality-soap operas *Temptation Island* or *Forever Eden*. "Forever"?—try never.

Love

The Abbott and Costello Show

You can take your Three Stooges—I'm an Abbott and Costello man. In particular, I'm an *Abbott and Costello Show* fan: this half-hour show, filmed between 1951 and 1953, contains everything their movies, radio shows, and stage acts did, including the consummately punned "Who's On First?" baseball routine, and distilled their comedy to its most potent form. Bud Abbott, angular, brusque, a straight man with a con man's smoothness and a raspy-rough voice, and Lou Costello, pudgy-soft, as round as the bowler atop his head, prone to wailing like a baby when scared, were a fast, abrasive team. They loved smack-your-hat-off slapstick and groaner puns: When they ran a pet store, Bud took a phone call, hung up and instructed Lou to go pick up an ailing "peek," or Pekinese pup. "Get a peek at Mrs. Pike," said Abbott. "Why can't I get a *good* look?" shot back Costello. That same episode, "Bingo's Troubles," contained a typical dash of ahead-of-their-time absurdism, literally. For once, Lou made Bud the victim: "Why don't ya answer the phone," Lou says. "The phone's not ringing," says Bud, and it's not. "Why wait 'til the last minute?" Lou insists. Bud begins to stare at him incomprehendingly . . . and the phone rings. Was it written that way? Was it an ad-lib for a missed sound-effect cue? Who knew? That was part of the fun.

In the TV show, depending on the week, they were always just one step ahead or behind on the rent to Mr. Fields—bald, angry Sid Fields—who also wrote a few of the scripts, and Lou pined for the tall, willowy Hillary Brooke. The series, filmed in front of a live audience, had essentially two sets, the boys' apartment house, and the front stoop of the building. Out on the street could be found easily riled Mike the Cop (Gordon Jones) and most oddly, Stinky, an overgrown child dressed in a Little Lord Fauntleroy suit. He was played with bizarre and headlong conviction by Joe Besser—yes, I know: he was one of the numerous "third Stooge"s, but this was his great role. He was the prissy sissy-boy who, when teased by Lou, always squealed, "I'm gonna *hit* you!"

The plots were minimal—Lou gets mistaken for a mobster's boyfriend; Bud tells Lou to stay in their apartment so Mr. Fields can't lock them out; the boys take care of a monkey, Bingo, a semiregular until he was canned after biting Costello. All that mattered were the two of them. They could talk about anything and befuddle each other, like a couple who'd been together forever.

"Once when I was hunting, there was thunder and lightning and these big animals with horns came by," Lou would say.

"Reindeer?" asks Bud.

"You bet, honey," says Lou sweetly.

Sheer bliss . . .

Hate

Rowan & Martin's Laugh-In: It Sure Wasn't Any *Hee Haw*

Premiering in 1968, *Rowan & Martin's Laugh-In* on NBC bridged a cultural gap at a volatile time. Dan Rowan and Dick Martin were a nightclub act—a *very* poor man's Martin and Lewis—who brought their tuxes and their smirks to the service of producer George Schlatter. He wanted to revive vaudeville-theater-style, black-out comedy: quick sketches, unrelated to each other, with a bunch of curvy girls hanging around to dance, be dumb, or get hit ("Sock it to me!").

But Schlatter was also smart enough to know that such an old-fashioned concept was running up against the flowering counterculture and a real world that was immersed in the Vietnam War. So, mass entertainer that he was, he used Rowan and Martin's conventional presentation as the audience's surrogate—the duo would do an opening comedy bit and then enter the show's "party scene," where cast regulars like Goldie Hawn, Arte Johnson, Ruth Buzzi, and Jo Anne Worley would booglaoo for a bit, then everyone would freeze, and the camera would zoom in on a comic who'd utter a one-liner like, "We'll never win the War on Poverty until all those poor people surrender."

Note that that line (uttered in February 1968 by Worley) referenced Lyndon Johnson's social program. *Laugh-In* was filled with political commentary; nearly all of it, because of the times, would now be considered liberal. Even Rowan and Martin were enlisted in the counterculture to some extent; playing sportscasters, they did a mock play-by-play of a college football game in which "students are kicking the president of Dow Chemical"—which *Laugh-In*'s audience would know was the then-villified manufacturer of napalm. "Penalty is immediate induction into the Army!" Martin yelled.

Laugh-In was less liberal about race. Prefiguring cable TV's "news-crawl," *Laugh-In* had its own, and it was likely to carry a line like, "Rap Brown . . . Then Rap Stokely Carmichael . . ." A black guest like Flip Wilson would look intimately into the camera and say conspiratorially, "When we take over, I'm gonna look out for you." You might say that *Laugh-In* was brave in expressing the country's racial tensions; you might also say that it ridiculed radicalism in the hope that it would go away.

You'd also have to say that the comedy was pretty awful. One groaner followed another ("Will the real Toulouse-Lautrec please stand up?"), and the show's catchphrases ("Sock it to me!" "You bet your sweet bippy!") were repeated over the seasons until they became irritating noise.

Laugh-In certainly isn't the revolutionary, or groundbreaking, or even funny show TV historians make it out to be. Much better is the show that premiered a year later, intended as a country-music-based rip-off of *Laugh-In*, CBS's *Hee Haw*. This was the much-despised series that replaced the cause-célèbre *Smothers Brothers Comedy Hour* in June of 1969. Despised, that is, by city-slicker TV-critic snobs who wouldn't have known George Jones from Grandpa Jones. The latter was a first-rate banjo player and mountain-music comedian who was a regular on this intentionally cornpone show; instead of popping out of Day-Glo–colored windows to deliver their one-liners, the Hee Haw gang, which included hosts Buck Owens and Roy Clark, Archie Campbell, Minnie Pearl, and Gordie Tapp, leapt up out of an overgrown cardboard cornfield to deliver their howlers.

The thing is, *Hee Haw*'s hosts were a lot more talented than *Laugh-In*'s: Clark was a deft multi-instrumentalist, and Owens was a bona-fide country music pioneer—the architect of the so-called Bakersfield Sound, a plaintive but driving honky-tonk sound honed not in Nashville but in the working-class bars of Bakersfield, California. Moreover, the stock company was a lot more skilled at delivering punchlines, too. Pearl and Grandpa Jones were vets of the Grand

Ole Opry, with literally decades' worth of material and timing at their command.

CBS cancelled *Hee Haw* after a mere two years—not because of poor ratings; it was in the Top Twenty when CBS axed a bunch of shows, mostly sitcoms like *Petticoat Junction,* in an effort to get a younger and more urban audience. When it went into syndication, *Hee Haw* ran for twenty-two years, and showcased a hell of a lot more talent both comedic—the late, gifted improvisor Gaillard Sartain is a man someone should write a long profile about some day—and musical. All the greats—George Jones, Tammy Wynette, Loretta Lynn, and Merle Haggard, to name just a few—stopped by to deliver terrific, full-length songs.

Laugh-In was a cynical ploy to make the audience feel superior to the culture that was changing all around them; *Hee Haw* was an idealistic playground where performers too often denied prime-time access were allowed to shine gloriously.

Love

Andy Rooney: Great Grump

Why is it that familiarity on television—perpetual reruns of decades-old shows—most often breeds affection for even the meretricious junk, but in some cases provokes hostility or dismissiveness far out of proportion to a show or a personality? Andy Rooney stands as a perfect example. As I wrote this book, I began telling people some of the "love" and "hate" entries. To a man and woman, every time I brought up Rooney's name, I heard something like, "Oh, God, don't you *hate* him?"

Jeez, no. Rooney may need to trim his out-of-control eyebrows more often, but other than that, I cannot think of a more fecund, lively, endlessly imaginative curmudgeon produced by the medium, and yes, I'm old enough to remember the marvelous Henry Morgan and young enough to know and despise the comedian and *Daily Show* contributor Lewis Black. Andy Rooney is, in a way, cursed by his success as the final ticker on *60 Minutes*; his and the show's very longevity has eroded the esteem with which he was once and still should be held.

Rooney started out in TV writing comedy for first-TV-generation performers like Gary Moore, Arthur Godfrey, Sam Levenson, and Victor Borge. Then he switched over to CBS News and formed a friendship with reporter/anchor Harry Reasoner. His CBS connection permitted him to write and produce the first evidence of his own brand of whimsy. One day, asked by CBS News president

Richard Salant, what he could do, Rooney boasted, "I can do any-thing; I can do—" he glanced around the office they were in "—I can do doors." He did: *An Essay On Doors,* an hour-long documen-tary, aired in '64. I couldn't track it down, but I'll bet Rooney's doc-umentary doors were more interesting than 99 percent of today's reality-TV human stars.

The Great American Dream Machine, a noble PBS folly combining news, criticism, and whimsy, 1971–1972, permitted Rooney to write, produce, and narrate more pointed, political visual essays. (To paraphrase George S. Kaufman, satire on TV is what gets cancelled after a season.) *Dream Machine* gave full voice to Rooney—a cranky, scratchy voice, full of curiosity about the world and wonderment that people didn't follow common sense. It was this sort of opin-ionated directness that led to *60 Minutes*; producer Don Hewitt hired Rooney to replace Jack Kilpatrick and Shana Alexander's "Point/ Counterpoint" segment after they became so boring even *Saturday Night Live* stopped parodying them. "A Few Minutes with Andy Rooney" was an immediate hit, controversial in its small way (people—including network bigwigs—get heated up over the darnedest things: a Rooney piece about toenail fungus was once spiked [or whatever they do in TV for killed pieces—erased?] be-cause his overseers found the subject unsavory) (which it is, but I'd still like to have heard what Andy Rooney had to say about such an uncomfortably mundane subject).

Over the years, being a professional opinionizer has gotten Rooney into trouble, mostly for remarks he's made not on *60 Minutes,* but off-the-cuff comments in interviews, as when, talking football on ESPN in 2002, he said, "The only thing that really bugs me about television's coverage is those damn women they have down on the sidelines who don't know what the hell they're talking about . . . I'm not a sexist person, but a woman has no business being down there trying to make some comment about a football game." Well, that's pretty foolish, of course, and the kind of thing that nowadays gets Rooney dismissed as a crank. If you go back and look at Rooney's often witty, even elegant, remarks ranging from war to the rise of the computer and the demise of the typewriter, he not only makes sense—he stands as the only truly good writer among the *60 Minutes* correspondents, better than all the marquee names that precede him on the show, from Mike Wallace, who made his rep with a trumped-up "gotcha!" style of TV tabloidism, to Ed Bradley, who made his rep as—what?—the first *60 Minutes* man to wear an earring?

Rooney's better than all of his *Minutes* costars. Someone should put his CBS and PBS documentary features on DVD, to help restore his image.

Hate

Viewers for Quality Television—Advocates of Middlebrow Uplift

Formed in 1984 to save that paragon of earnest pseudofeminist treacle, *Cagney & Lacey,* Viewers for Quality Television (VQT) was a grassroots organization of TV fans who lobbied networks and cable companies to keep them from cancelling poorly rated shows. For every show worthy of support, like *My So-Called Life,* VQT threw its light weight behind mediocrities like *Beauty and the Beast, Mad About You,* the *Star Trek* spin-offs, and *Grace Under Fire.* Beginning in a pre-e-mail era, founder Dorothy Swanson worked diligently to get VQT members to write in to networks, but as even she admitted in her 2000 book, *The Story of Viewers for Quality Television: Grassroots to Prime Time,* her group was often met with disdain, if not outright hostility, from the TV industry. VQT's efforts inevitably took the shape of form letters that were soon easily identified by television executives who'd been targeted for appeals and whiny threats of boycotts.

During the course of its sixteen years, VQT bestowed "Q" Awards granting their "seal of quality" upon a show; it was like putting a series in Tupperware and cutting off its air. Once you'd been recognized by VQT, whether your show was good or bad, it took on the aura of being something you should watch rather than want to watch: VQT was the spinach of pop-culture advocacy groups. Who needed VQT to hand out awards to shows like *China Beach,* highminded middlebrow commentary about the Vietnam War? VQT was not about to say that the reason lots of people watched was because they found Dana Delany and/or Marg Helgenberger easy on the eyes. Or to *Designing Women* or *Murphy Brown* long after those ladies had ceased to be even remotely funny or provocative? VQT never strayed far from the mainstream.

VQT died in 2001 having long before becoming irrelevant in an Internet world where a thousand Web sites could spring up overnight to rally 'round a cherished bit of programming. More significantly, the earnestness of VQT could not survive in the snarky world of 'neticism, where last night's *Buffy the Vampire Slayer* or *X-Files* episode was analyzed, evaluated, championed, condemned, and placed in an arbitrary ranking system with every other *Buffy* or *X-Files* episode.

In a larger sense, what died before 2001 was the notion of "quality" itself—something that was a necessary component of an enjoyable TV series. It's likely that HBO's *Mr. Show,* Chris Elliott's *Get a Life,* the live-action sitcom *The Tick,* or *Andy Richter Controls the Universe* would not, by VQT's standards, be considered "quality" shows. They were too obstreperous, too unruly, too unpredictable to merit the kind of stodgy, school marmish, give-it-a-gold-star attention Viewers for Quality Television lavished upon more obviously quality-with-a-capital-Q faves like *Brooklyn Bridge,* the Gary David Goldberg mawk-com, or *Brooklyn South,* the self-consciously "edgy" cop series. Viewers for Quirky Television: Now *there's* an organization that already exists, for anyone with a computer and the e-mail address of a network. It may not save any more shows that VQT did, but you'll sure have more fun, and feel less piously ignored or persecuted, than the old VQT crowd did. One thing TV is about is community, even when what we commune around is about to be cancelled. Righteous anger, not handing out awards or giving seals of approval, is often the best defense tactic. VQT: RIP.

Love

James Garner: All That Is Solid Melts into Air

First in *Maverick* (1957–1960) and then in *The Rockford Files* (1974–1980), James Garner did for hour-long television what Cary Grant did for the movies, bestowing upon the medium performances that come off as effortless, sly, and profoundly virile—at least in part because of his willingness to seem foolish, or even heartlessly amoral. No TV hero, when attacked, has been beaten up as regularly and resoundingly. No TV hero, when doing the attacking, has so often sucker-punched his menacing-stooge attackers.

As Bret Maverick, Garner was a crooked gambler with a suitably crooked grin. The show's creator, Roy Huggins, said the series, premiering at the height of the TV Western's popularity in the late '50s, was conceived to be "exactly the opposite" of such traditional oaters as *Gunsmoke* and *Bonanza*. Maverick wore a fancy but dusty black suit and hat (black hats had heretofore signified "villain" to the viewer), and he drifted from town to town, card-sharping the locals in countless saloon. Huggins called Maverick "a gentle grafter" in his original guide notes for writers for the series. Even more self-consciously significant, Huggins dubbed his character "a happy existentialist" whose "motives always derive from himself, never from others, or from the 'community.'"

The role was made, in other words, for Garner's jaundiced wink. Possessed of the handsomeness usually called rugged, Garner was trying to launch a feature-film career when *Maverick* came along—

in fact, he'd just been cast as Marlon Brando's sidekick in *Sayonara* in 1957 when his contract with Warner Bros. studios obliged him to do the *Maverick* pilot. Garner complied with his TV masters, and so his small-screen stardom began out of frustration and regret. Viewers were not only beguiled by Garner's lovable-rogue character, but they also enjoyed the way *Maverick* pissed on other Westerns. In one clever little parody of *Bonanza*, an episode called "Three Queens Full," Bart rescues three unwillingly chosen brides destined for rancher Joe Wheelwright's trio of peculiar sons, Moose, Henry, and Small Paul. (FYI for post-boomers: *Bonanza* was about Lorne Greene's Ben Cartwright and his sons Hoss, Adam, and Little Joe.)

After *Maverick*, Garner tried relaunching a film career and came up short. Slinking back to TV, he starred in an interesting one-season flop, *Nichols* (1971–1972)—people didn't want to see their man as a shabby frontier hobo who travelled around with his droopy dog. So Garner re-upped with Huggins for *The Rockford Files*—again, a subversion of a genre, this time the private-eye saga, then at the height of its TV popularity. Jim Rockford was a half-decent private detective in Los Angeles—the opening credits flashed images of the Bel Air hotel and a Ventura Freeway exit sign. But Rockford wasn't a cool-cat investigator like the sharkskin-suit demi–Rat Packers on *Peter Gunn* or *77 Sunset Strip*; he operated out of a tidy, and therefore all the more depressing, trailer home. Huggins signalled his break with the genre's tradition right in the opening credits. Instead of employing the standard leggy secretary to field his clients, Rockford had a big, clunky answering machine clicking on to screen his calls. The machine was shown at the start of every episode.

Jim Rockford had the L.A. version of Bret Maverick's wannabe fashion sense—he invariably wore an open necked dress shirt and the same natty-but-frayed hound's-tooth check sport jacket—and took on clients who couldn't afford better-dressed dicks. It's impossible to watch Garner in *Rockford* and not sense that at least some of the periodic sourness in his character derived from the actor's own frustration at having spent the better part of a decade trying to become a feature-film leading man. Indeed, he'd already tried his hand at Raymond Chandler's *ne plus ultra* of detectives in the title role of 1969 *Marlowe*, a drab version of Chandler's most underrated novel, *The Little Sister*.

But Chandler, with his flashy similes and pretensions to swank, wasn't the right source material for Garner anyway. His Jim Rockford was more a character out of novels by Ross Macdonald (haunted by family in the person of his affable but nagging father; attracted to cases involving adolescent runaways or men his own age who'd hit the wall of midlife crisis) and Donald Westlake (comic capers that turn violent with the flash of a gun muzzle). *Rockford Files*, among whose writer-producers was future *Sopranos* creator David Chase, was a perfect showcase for Garner's unique projection of craggy handsomeness and canny cowardice. The show surrounded the star with good scenery-chewing character actors and a costar like Noah Beery, Jr., as Rockford's irascible, junkyard dog of a dad, Jim's nightmare version of himself twenty years down the line, and a good motivation to keep taking cases that might lift his status in life. *The Rockford Files* was also written a notch above other private-eye shows, with a colorful squawk and cyncism. In one episode, Sam Peckinpah–stock-player Strother Martin, playing a wild-haired old coot Rockford is hired to spring from a phony mental hospital, yawps to a nurse, "You're not gonna electroshock me, ya barren queen!" Nobody ever talked like this on *Cagney & Lacey.*

You can see Garner's influence in later TV stars—David Duchovny's sexy underdoggedness in *The X-Files*; George Clooney's insouciant doctoring in *ER*. Highly praised, minimally rewarded—a single Emmy for the star in '77—Garner remains TV's best light comedian. Ever.

Hate

The Simple Life: The Rich Are Not Like Us

It started out, in 2003, as a concept that would level the *Green Acres* playing field: Socialite brats Paris Hilton and Nicole Richie, separated from their cash and credit cards by Fox on *The Simple Life*, were dispatched to rural America, there to be shaken out of their pampered complacency by ordinary folks unimpressed with the pair's tabloid notoriety. After all, where else would the entertainment come from if the girls didn't truly engage with "the simple life"?

Well, turns out the series devolved into a weekly half hour that could have been called *Let's Sneer at the Hicks*. Paris and Nicole imposed their condescending rudeness and sense of privilege upon everyone they met. Ostensibly silly fun, a variation on *The Osbornes* in the venerable aren't-the-rich-out-of-touch? genre, *The Simple Life* and its popularity instead signalled more of a cultural shift than I'd anticipated: Americans used to identify with ordinary people and laugh when the high-and-mighty were brought low. Now, apparently, an awful lot of us just want Paris Hilton's credit-card limit and find ordinary folk to be contemptible squares who don't understand that the trick to life is getting away with as much as you can.

Paris and Nicole whine and flirt, shake their groove things and wheedle cash for highway tolls and gas from young men who are in on the now nationally known joke but too polite or embarrassed not to hand over a few bills. It's all as nauseating as watching men stuff twenties into strippers' G-strings, except those girls work a lot harder than P and N. And TV couldn't wait to exploit these exploiters of the masses even more. Networks signed up Paris's mom to do a reality show in which she guides young ladies luckless enough not to have married a hotel heir as she did in the finer points of etiquette and the attainment of, as her NBC show has it, *The Good Life.*

And Paris's father Rick has executive-produced a show called *777*—the payoff number on slot machines—that would put seven high-rollers gamblers together in a Vegas suite and compete in a series of games for a prize of $7 million. That this is probably what Rick hands his daughter annually as a shoe allowance only adds to the undercurrent of repulsiveness.

Unlike James Garner—all natural ease, portraying in his prime con men who wink and beguile—the Hiltons are arrogant hustlers, exceedingly bad actors in their own reality scenarios, yet lacking even the knavish wiles that make Garner and his Bret Maverick and his Jim Rockford such satisfying salts of the earth.

Love

Homicide's Best Cop and Its Best Villain

Homicide: Life on the Street (1993–1999) earned most of its rave reviews the good ol' TV-critic way: by producing initially strong first seasons, showily "good" acting, attracting only moderate ratings, and coming from a certain pool of critics'-darling producer-writers. In this case, Tom Fontana had been part of the *St. Elsewhere* high-middlebrow graduate school that included Mark Tinker and the late Bruce Paltrow. If Andre Braugher's performance as the terse, uptight Det. Frank Pembleton was justly hailed and then rapidly overrated as his granite line readings ossified, two other performances in this series are vastly underrated, by actors who purely coincidentally share a common bond—raised by parents of the '60s counterculture.

The first is Clark Johnson's Meldrick Lewis, the porkpie-hatted black cop who came on loose and affable, a slightly Southern twang and slur in this Baltimore investigator's voice. Lewis rarely got the showy scenes that Braugher and Kyle Secor did, but when Meldrick went into "the box"—the interrogation room—with a suspect, he was a masterful bully, all the more surprising to his quarry for initially appearing to be so easygoing.

Johnson has also proven a worthy director. His 2001 HBO movie *Boycott,* starring Jeffrey Wright (*Angels in America*) as Dr. Martin Luther King, Jr., is one of the finest movies ever made about a black leader in America. Johnson manages to portray King as a complicated, flawed, yet never less than heroic man, and, more crucially, to place him in the context of his time without applying the hindsight coating of sociological/pop-entertainment-of-the-moment shellac that so often mars biopics.

Speaking of someone with a historical context brings me to *Homicide*'s greatest villain: Erik Todd Dellums as the slithery drug dealer Luther Mahoney. Mahoney, who figured in a number of episodes scattered throughout the series, was a cut above the usual *Homicide* baddie. No street dealer or thug-pimp, Mahoney was a preternaturally calm, hyper-articulate overlord of narcotics distribution. He'd have made a worthy candidate for some turf tussles with Tony Soprano over on HBO.

Like Clark Johnson, whose mother was a Black Panther, Dellums is the son of radical politics—specifically, the son of former California House of Representatives member Ron Dellums, one of the fiercest and most eloquent denouncers of the Vietnam War. A decorated military veteran, Dellums *père* accused the United States of "war crimes" and in 1980 declared, "We should totally dismantle every intelligence agency in this country piece by piece, brick by brick, nail by nail." Erik—the middle son of three Dellums children—took a political science degree from Brown and worked for a semester for then–House speaker Tip O'Neill. Other than appearing in *Good to Go*, a cheap but fun 1986 movie about D.C.'s "go-go music" scene (can I get a hand for Chuck Brown and the Soul Searchers, anyone?) and small parts in a couple of Spike Lee films, Erik seems not to have inherited a yen for political life, although you could say that his portrayal of Luther Mahoney on *Homicide: Life on the Street* is a form of actorly agit-prop: He never lets you forget that, as bad a man as Luther is, the context of his existence—his "life on the street"—forced a brilliant young mind to turn to criminal pursuits as surely as Johnson's Meldrick Lewis decided to take his tough upbringing and bring wayward men like Luther to justice.

In both cases, we are treated to performances by black actors equal or superior to any that could be seen on the screen or on the stage during *Homicide*'s TV run.

Hate

Don't Confuse Your Conrads: William Was the Fat One, Robert Was the Fatuous One

You young'uns who hope to get a grasp on your TV history are always making this mistake, I've heard it a hundred times, getting your Conrads mixed up. Pay attention:

William Conrad was a pretty lovable guy (I mean, on-screen; who knows, maybe he was, as Austin Powers would say, a "fat bastard" off-camera) whom many of you know as the star of two unlikely but popular series. The first was *Cannon* (1971–1976), in which he played Frank Cannon, a L.A. detective who, after the first season, could barely heave his frame out of his car to catch a perp. That's why a lot of people liked him: He was super-sized before super-sizing was cool. His second hit was the crappier *Jake and the Fatman* (1987–1992), in which the mustachioed Conrad teamed with pretty-boy muscle-bunny Joe Penny as a D.A. and his investigator, respectively. Many people also recognize Conrad's extensive voiceover work in commercials and as the narrator of the David Janssen series *The Fugitive* and the *Rocky and Bullwinkle* cartoons. Fewer realize that Conrad also directed some episodes of such good TV shows as *Gun-*

smoke and *The Rifleman*. He made a pretty good TV Nero Wolfe. He croaked in 1994.

Now, the Conrad we *hate* is *Robert* Conrad, the insufferably cocky jerk who starred most famously in the gimmicky, James Bond-in-the-frontier series *The Wild Wild West* (1965–1969), before that as a cocky jerk in the detective series *Hawaiian Eye* from 1959–1963, and after that as the *really* annoying cocky jerk in the 1976–1978 series *Baa Baa Black Sheep*, in which he played Pappy Boyington, leader of a group of fighter pilots. Conrad was the kind of high-school jock who prided himself on doing his own stunts, who made life hell for ordinary celebs as the hectoring captain of too many *Battle of the Network Stars* competitions in the '70s. He once made poor, rotund Donna Pescow (*Saturday Night Fever*) cry after losing, like, a swimming competition or something.

Conrad was a proud conservative (before entering show biz, he was fired from a job on the docks of Detroit in the '50s for trying to get his union steward fired) who always went on talk shows gassing on about the importance of morality and family; he played off his macho image in a series of battery commercials in which he dared you to knock one of the little items off his shoulder. "Go'wan—I dare ya!" he'd bark. Robert Conrad was a mean bully. Screw him.

Love

Buffalo Bill: The Great Misanthrope

In 1987, producer-writer Jay Tarses came up with *The Days and Nights of Molly Dodd*, starring a luminous Blair Brown as a single New York woman. Molly started out plucky and alluring. Her subdued affairs, conducted initially on NBC, are enthrallingly quaint and as intricately discreet as the romances in a Jane Austen novel when compared to the fuck-and-run antics of the soon-to-ensue *Sex and the City* on HBO. She ended up on the Lifetime network due to a combination of subtle acting and poor ratings. On that channel, Molly's context changed: She was just the sort of sad-sack singleton-with-baby that that cabler embraced all too wholeheartedly. The series was a critical darling, and its female fan base waged furious campaigns to keep the increasingly weepy-looking Molly (even *she* seemed tired of her goodness and her loneliness) on the air.

Molly can now be seen as Tarses's penance for what he'd done five years before. He unleashed Dabney Coleman, until that time a moderately well-known character actor best known as the mean boss in the 1980 Dolly Parton film *Nine to Five*, as "Buffalo" Bill Bittinger, as gleefully amoral a character as ever had a sitcom named after him. *Buffalo Bill*, which ran on NBC from May to August of '83, then from December to April of '84—an oh-so-grand total of seven months—captured the olive-pit black hearts of some critics, but it had no sizable support from print or public. Its passing was as lonely as Bill at home with a bottle of scotch his only companion on a Saturday night. But my, what a few terrific months it was. Buffalo Bill was a bitter, furiously angry, middle-aged crazy, the popular host of a Buffalo, New York, talk show who was convinced he'd been destined for greater stardom and decided to take his small-market fate out on his coworkers. At the time, reviewers regularly referred to the Bill character as being "*inexplicably* popular" in the context of the show-within-the-show, but now, all you have to do is take a look at Bill O'Reilly to understand that the public can easily affix its affection on angry, undeservingly bitter middle-aged men.

Buffalo Bill may have peaked with an episode in which Bill, on a whim, callously fires his black, Vietnam-vet makeup man played by Charles Robinson, who'd go on to longer employment on the hideous laugh-beggar *Night Court*. Bill then suffers a nightmare in which he's chased by spear-brandishing, racist-stereotypical "Zulu" warriors to the music of Ray Charles's "Hit the Road, Jack." The series can now be viewed as a precursor to Gary Shandling's insecure-egomaniac of *The Larry Sanders Show* and Larry David's anti-p.c. *Curb Your Enthusiasm*. Clearly, *Buffalo Bill* belonged on HBO as a sustained exercise in foul-tempered humor. The series contains Coleman's finest work. He makes utterly no effort to ingratiate himself to the studio or home audience; half the laughs seem more like gasps of shock. *Buffalo Bill* also extracted the best work from both Joanna Cassidy (now best known as Rachel Griffiths's garish mother on *Six Feet Under*) as *Bill* producer and half-willing, half-repelled paramour, and Geena Davis as a callow production assistant.

Three years later, Tarses and Coleman, who rightly, stubbornly, loved the persona they'd created, tried a modified version of it with *The "Slap" Maxwell Story*, about a crusty sportswriter whose roughhouse newspaper lifestyle no longer fit into the day's more superficially mannerly media world. It was a good idea with a ripe kernel of media criticism that was ahead of its time, but even a slightly softened Coleman wasn't nearly as funny. Slap was more vulnerable a man than Bill was, more aware of how out-of-step he was even if he couldn't resist a verbal slap shot or two. To a nun coaching a high-school basketball team, he said, "Y'know, Sister, you won't be able to hide behind that mustache forever . . ." It was Buffalo Bill's furious self-delusion, his persistence in being true to his own warped code of saying whatever popped into his head as a sign of integrity, that elevates him into a pantheon that can include both Ralph Kramden and George Costanza, that got his series cancelled so quickly, and helped make Tarses pretty much unemployable after *Molly Dodd*. *Buffalo Bill* remains a buried TV treasure; you'd think, at the very least, Tarses's daughter, television exec Jamie Tarses, could pull some strings to help get the show on DVD.

Hate

M*A*S*H: aka, *Most*Astonishingly overrated*Sitcom in*History*

In 1970, Robert Altman made a silly, dishevelled comedy based on Richard Hooker's silly, windbag comic novel about Korean War medics. The movie exploited that '50s military conflict for then-current anti–Vietnam war sentiment. Stars Elliott Gould and Donald Sutherland ambled through the proceedings like a stoned Hope-and-Crosby comedy team, tossing off muttered asides that passed for hipsterisms and which made the ticket-buyers feel privy— and superior—to the privates fighting a real war. The movie's stylistic flourish was to bring Altman's overlapping-dialogue mannerism to a broader audience when his *M*A*S*H* turned into a surprise box office hit.

Adapting the movie for TV in 1972 was Larry Gelbart, a former writer for Sid Caesar, among others, but a jokesmith with pretensions to social commentary. In Gelbart's version of *M*A*S*H,* the rebellious surgeons Hawkeye (Alan Alda) and Trapper John (Wayne Rogers) engaged in constant piously poignant punchlines. Like Hope and Crosby, Hawkeye and Trapper were golfers. This enabled Alda to utter lines in one of the series's recurring devices, maudlin letters to his father spoken as voiceover commentary, such as, "Dad, we try to play par surgery on this course—par is a live patient." Oooh, prime-time irony! In the pilot episode, the two golfing buddies tee off near camp and their ball hits a land mine: ka-*boom*! Oooh—the nearness of death!

Gelbart, who was also one of the series' executive producers, thought so highly of his own high-minded banalities that he fought CBS to keep a laugh track off the show. He lost that battle, with one small, odd, network semisurrender. CBS agreed to keep the laugh track out of the operating-room scenes, to let the jokes and blood fly, sending out the subconscious, contradictory message that imminent death was no laughing matter. The network was probably right about its laugh-track decision in general, however: without the canned chuckles, it's dubious that viewers in the early years of *M*A*S*H* would have recognized nearly meaningless lines like Hawkeye's challenge to stiff-necked surgeon Frank Burns (Larry Linville) to a duel—"specimen bottles at twenty paces!"—as a joke. After the series won a slew of Emmys and transformed Alda from ski-nosed wisecracker (he really was the liberal heir to Hope, wasn't he?) into a feminist talk-show bore, Gelbart was granted his laugh-track-free wish when he created another show, *United States* in 1980. This was a two-person comedy about a married couple (Beau Bridges and Helen Shaver) whose dialogue its author thought was so freighted with Meaning Beyond Humor that it should not be smeared with studio-larded laughter. The result? The silences after the duo's thudding punchlines (you could watch them pause for the laughter they assumed was erupting all across the, um, United States) only confirmed *United States*'s sense of its own smug self-importance (a fraught marriage as a metaphor for nothing less than America itself). The show was cancelled after two months.

United States only reemphasized the dubious legacy of *M*A*S*H:* that a truly worthy sitcom had to have something to say, some moral uplift—as opposed to, say, the Emmy-less but far more socially nuanced brilliance of *The Honeymooners*.

In interviews Gelbart disdained Altman's movie as lacking the former's showy subversiveness, and depending on which Altman interview you read, the director either "never watched" or detested the hamfisted, pun-infested, minimorality play Gelbart had turned the movie into. Nowadays, you can get DVDs of *M*A*S*H* that offer the option of turning off the laugh track to hear the show the way Gelbart and Co. intended—apparently, as a mirthless critique of American foreign policy capped by burlesque sex jokes (Hawkeye to Loretta Swit's Hot Lips Houlihan, in the operating room: "If you don't move, I'm gonna have to cut around your B-cups"). To paraphrase the show's awful title song, suicide is less painful.

Love

Oh Really?: Bill O'Reilly and *The O'Reilly Factor*

Where are all the great old-fashioned TV "personalities," the elder among you ask? Where's the Arthur Godfrey, the Art Linkletter, who unites a broad audience with folksy charm? Where, the less-elder among you ask, is the TV performer who is unafraid to alienate, unafraid to express a divisive opinion lest it rile a demographic—the latter kind of thinking so commonly held that it produces both Larry King and Ryan Seacrest? I would say that Bill O'Reilly is that personality. He is at once arrogant and avuncular; ruthlessly aggressive and assiduously polite; shameless and racked with shame; a know-it-all liar and a knowing television communicator. He is at once imperial and insecure, for what else is it but a paradoxical impulse that compels a man to refer to himself as "The Factor," a plug for his Fox News Channel show and an assertion that he is a player, a *factor*, in American culture?

It amazes me when I encounter people unimpressed by O'Reilly's achievement. Leave aside the massaged-over bio that tranforms this middle-class Levittown, New York, businessman's son into a working-class tough. By achievement, I'm talking about a guy who was low down on the TV totem pole—a "senior correspondent" on the late-'80s/early-'90s *Inside Edition*—who got really low-down—and dirty—by asserting his presence as a Factor in the public discourse, first on TV in 1996, then on radio in 2000. Hewing to a conservative/libertarian/populist/Ayn Randy–Objectivist ideology that renders his views both vehement and unpredictable (politically hawkish, social-issue squishy), O'Reilly has built an enormous following. For all his Web-page savvy, his popularity is constructed on the same elements that made radio-to-TV personalities like Godfrey a mass-appeal-pleaser in the '50s: The guy talks directly to *you*—it's one-on-one communication, confiding and seductive: O'Reilly is a communicator of the first rank.

Of course, he's also a jerk of the first rank. I disagree vehemently with him: Would I be an East Coast media critic if I didn't? Of *course* I think his "no-spin zone" shtick is, well, shtick, but it's also an admirably effective hook. His TV show is brilliantly produced. The opening monologue goes against fundamental TV rules: He raises numerous topics, and prints text on the screen—you read along with him. This is at once as revolutionary and as old-fashioned as TV gets. He's one step away from asking fans to put a sheet of plastic on the screen and draw pictures with him, the way the old *Winky Dink* kid's show used to a half-century ago. (Ask your parents, Gens X, Y, and Z.)

Having appeared on O'Reilly's TV and radio shows as an attacked guest, I can attest to the man's impeccable manners, both on- and off-screen. Sure, O'Reilly is, as a poster says on his Web site, a "blowhard." But the point there is, O'Reilly *lets people post that he's a blowhard.* He knows that the best way to disarm your foes is to invite them into your lair. In a media world filled with the timid and the lame, Bill O'Reilly—love him, hate him, attack him, but don't, he admirably insists, idolize him—is the sort of strong-willed presence television needs more of, but with opposing views. I'm not holding my breath for the progressive version of O'Reilly, but he remains, um, a factor in my thinking about what TV should be.

Hate

Geraldo Rivera

This one is like shooting fish in a barrel, you say—who doesn't hate the showboating "news"-man who hosted the live show that opened Al Capone's long-sealed vault only to reveal . . . bupkes? Whose daytime garbage-scow—'scuse me, talk-show—*Geraldo* provoked a 1988 fight among Aryan Nation youths and black activist Roy Innis, resulting in a broken-nose Rivera proudly stuck into the nation's face for weeks later? Who published an autobiography called *Exposing Myself* in which he claimed to had bedded "thousands" of women including Bette Midler and Liza Minnelli? Who, in a related detail, incurred the wrath of novelist—and father-in-law—Kurt Vonnegut by cheating on his daughter, Edith?

Rivera certainly makes it easy to forget that he began his career as a true crusader while a local reporter for New York City's WABC-TV News, whose report on the dreadful conditions at the Willowbrook State School for the mentally ill won awards, and led to a government investigation that resulted in the shutdown of that disgraceful institution.

That's about all that can be said for him, however. Rivera has placed himself in dangerous situations as a war correspondent who has been, as his Fox News Channel biography puts it, "on the frontlines in virtually every international conflict since 1973." But to what end? There is no eloquence to Rivera's reporting; he was even expelled from Iraq in 2003 by the U.S. military for "giving away crucial details of future military operations during a live broadcast." Before that, the *Baltimore Sun* accused Rivera of lying about being at the scene of a "friendly fire" incident in Afghanistan, a charge he has vigorously denied. His reports have neither a point of view nor a philosophy. He expresses no curiosity these days about the suffering of others—he's a traveller, a risk-taker, but this ain't no George Orwell. He's one of the reasons people don't place much store in TV news. He's a bad joke who's in it for the money and the fame and nothing else.

Love

Miami Vice, Crime Story, and *Robbery Homicide Division:*
Michael Mann's Great Hard-Boiled Trilogy

Before he started spattering blood across the screen in the most elegantly moody way possible in films such as *The Last of the Mohicans, Heat, Manhunter* (the *real Silence of the Lambs*), and *Collateral,* Michael Mann was a TV guy. As an up-and-comer, he wrote episodes of *Starsky and Hutch* and *Bronk,* the latter the one-season, mid-'70s cop show that tried to turn Jack Palance into a TV star. He co-created and wrote episodes of the uber–Robert Urich series, *Vega$.* In 1979, Mann wrote and directed one of the most tersely suspenseful TV-movies ever made, *The Jericho Mile,* a prison drama starring Peter Strauss. The success of *Jericho* gave him the juice to launch his directorial feature-film career with 1981's *Thief* starring a stoic James Caan, a beautifully ravaged Tuesday Weld, and eerie heist-music by Tangerine Dream.

Mann is no media snob. He moves back and forth between TV and film, and in *Miami Vice* (1984–1989), co-created by Anthony Yerkovich, Mann hit the jackpot. Bursting with the visual paradox of creating a bright-hued *noir* (stars Don Johnson and Philip Michael Thomas strutted around busting perps wearing flamingo-pinks, sand-dune beiges, and blinding-sun-white jackets—no socks, please!), the series made a rainbow splash for its fashion style, for Johnson and Thomas's Crockett-and-Stubbs banter, for Jan Hammer's percussive theme music, and for the way it used rock music.

One entire song by a big-name star was usually featured per episode. Legend has it that the series was sold to NBC with a mere phrase— "MTV cops"—and the novelty of the music was such that, in this pre-Internet era, newspapers published the name of song and artist the day after the show aired. More important to Mann was the fact that *Vice* was also pervaded by an abundance of his feature films' philosophy: the pursuit of power as a telltale sign of moral rot.

Flush with *Vice* money, Mann launched *Crime Story* in 1986. He was the show's executive producer, and if he wasn't as hands-on as he'd been with *Vice*, it looked like a Mann creation from top (Dennis Farina, once a real-life Chicago cop, played a break-the-rules 1960s Chicago cop) to bottom (Del Shannon was coaxed out of retirement to redo "Runaway" as a TV theme!). *Crime Story* only lasted two seasons, but it remains a slick cult item, highly watchable for Farina's sharklike forward momentum as Lt. Mike Torello, and for stage actor Stephen Lang's turn as a shrewd, bespectacled attorney. Around the edges, watch for future *Once & Again* star Billy Campbell as a callow cop and Andrew (no-"Dice") Clay as a hoodlum stooge.

After shooting the criminally neglected 1989 TV-movie *L.A. Takedown*, which would become the template for Mann's great DeNiro-Pacino feature *Heat*, Mann tried another TV series. *Robbery Homicide Division* should have been—and in some ways is—the culmination of Mann's TV work . . . if only it hadn't been cancelled after barely limping across the 2002–2003 season. As he did in *Crime Story*, Mann again evinced a fondness for using a big, atypically bullish man as his hero. Tom Sizemore played Lt. Sam Cole as though he was going to lunge at the camera and throttle anyone who got in his way. Mann pioneered a new way of shooting a cop series, taking relatively small digital cameras out into the seedier sections of Los Angeles, using a lot of natural night light (neon, car headlights) to achieve an eerily surreal yet speedy effect.

RHD may not have been particularly original in its story material—goons commit crime; Sizemore's crew hunts them down—but like everything Mann does, it had an arresting look, an uncompromising narrative method, and a terrific lead performance from Sizemore: wisecracking yet moody, a feral loner capable of great sensitivity. In other words, Sizemore was the perfect Mann hero: solitary, bold, tight-lipped, capable of violence. (Unfortunately, this concept spilled over into newspaper headlines when Sizemore himself was accused of battering his girlfriend, the former madam-to-the-stars Heidi Fleiss.)

RHD had all the makings of a great TV show except decent ratings. It suffered on CBS from invidious comparisons to *CSI*, the procedural style of which was just beginning to attract a large viewership and would therefore set the tone for other crime shows. Mann, an original artist above all else, would never have compromised *Robbery Homicide Division* to accommodate changes, and so it joins *Crime Story* as a cult classic and a worthy third chapter in Mann's TV trilogy.

Hate

Made-for-TV Movies and Miniseries

There has been exactly one great American made-for-television movie: *Lonesome Dove*, the 1989 adaptation of Larry McMurtry's novel, starring Robert Duvall and Tommy Lee Jones as cussed, itching, horny cowboys on a cattle drive from Texas to Montana. Former Texas Rangers, Duvall's chatty Gus McCrae and Jones's taciturn Woodrow Call share an easy friendship belied by the uneasy feeling that their best days are gone, that this cattle drive may be their last, and that the old West they knew is vanishing. That last point was echoed in the TV industry, where producer Suzanne DePasse, who'd bought the rights to McMurtry's bestseller, encountered pop-culture wisdom—that the Western was dead. She proved everyone wrong. *Dove* got great reviews and ratings, and, as directed by Simon Wincer, the six-hour, four-part miniseries lifted the game of TV vet Robert Urich as raffish gambler Jake Spoon and rebirthed the career of one-time kid star Rick Schroeder, portraying callow Newt Dobbs.

Before and after *Lonesome Dove*, the history of the TV movie is overwhelmingly pathetic. Originally conceived in the '70s by the television industry as a relatively inexpensive way to compete with theatrical films, the average TV movie cost about $750,000 to make back then. You'd think the format would have been the breeding ground for young directors, writers, and actors to use the fast-and-cheap ethos to make the TV equivalent of good, unpretentious B movies. Instead of breeding a small-screen generation of Sam Fullers (*The Steel Helmet*) and Budd Boettichers (*Ride Lonesome*)—directors who knew how to use small budgets to make small genre pictures with stark emotional power—the TV industry did what it knows best: going for middlebrow uplift, for soap-opera tearjerkers, for British imports, and for American damaged goods.

The first wave of miniseries brought forth the rise of PBS's *Masterpiece Theatre* with the premiere of *The Forsyte Saga* (1967) and, more crucially, *Roots* (1977), the eight-night, twelve-hour mini that portrayed the American slave trade with the ham-fisted melodrama of a grandly produced high-school pageant. The popularity and critical raves for *Forsyte* carried the crippling implication that anything based on literature, even sudsy lit like John Galsworthy's, was superior to an original teleplay. *Roots*, with its record-breaking ratings and profoundly serious subject matter reduced to likable victim-heroes and florid, hiss-boo villains, defined the TV movie and miniseries, forever dooming it to mediocrity.

The marquee attractions wedged into our living rooms tended to veer between adaptations of crappy books like *The Thorn Birds* (1983) and *Shogun* (1980)—aka *Richard Chamberlain's Greatest Hits*—or ostentatiously "bold" forays into profoundly serious subjects like *Holocaust* (1978). Writing about the latter, which starred a young Meryl Streep, the critic Clive James noted that "no character existed nor action took place except to make a point." This is precisely why so many TV movies are so awful. Well, that, and the fact that so many of them are so long. The eighteen hours of *The Winds of War* (1983) and its *thirty-hour* sequel, *War and Remembrance* (1988), forced some of us to make the poor-taste joke that sitting through both seemed longer than World War II. Based on sludgy bestseller fiction by Herman Wouk and starring Robert Mitchum, one of many top-notch film stars who went, like so many woolly mastodons, to the miniseries format to live out their final, waning years, these wars were punishing insults to history, its heroes, and its victims.

Speaking of victims, the TV-movie genre also gave rise to the so-called "disease of the week" and "women in jeopardy" genres—again, dreadful reductions of complex, often tragic, subjects like AIDS and spouse-abuse. Occasionally a good, shrewd TV-movie would surface, like 1981's *Murder in Texas*, starring Farrah Fawcett and Sam Elliott in a crackerjack junk-thriller. Then Fawcett felt compelled to do unnecessary image-rehabilitation by putting herself through the agony of *The Burning Bed* (1984), in which Paul LeMat beat her senseless in a two-hour admonition that there were men out there who deserved to be put way, if not simply killed, for the way they treat women. This was TV as public-service announcement, but it came across in sappy reviews and among viewers looking to justify their taste as Important Television.

The Brits do this genre better—or at least one did: writer Dennis Potter, whose atypically constructed *Pennies From Heaven* and *The Singing Detective* put 99 percent of all American TV movies and miniseries to shame. Given how many of these things our country produces, it's inevitable that an occasional first-rate one will emerge now and then, like director Michael Ritchie's wonderfully corrosive media satire *The Positively True Adventures of the Alleged Texas Cheerleader-Murdering Mom* (1993), starring Holly Hunter. But the vast majority of made-for-TV films are worthless tripe, and like the tripe that comes from the belly of an ox, long and tasteless as well.

Love

Don't Mess with Marg Helgenberger

No TV actress has embodied the ol' madonna/whore paradox more literally and figuratively than Marg Helgenberger. Trained in the soaps (*Ryan's Hope*, 1928–1986), the Nebraska-born actress never looked corn-fed—whether portraying the Vietnam-era hooker/ heroin addict/abandoning mother in her thirties on *China Beach* (1988–1991) or the contemporary forensic investigator/ex-stripper/ single mom in her forties on *CSI*, Helgenberger is distinctive. No merely pretty strawberry-blonde, she has a haunted look that manifests itself in her crafty eyes, her gaunt cheekbones, her smokey yet sharp voice. In an earlier era, she'd have been compared to Ida Lupino, another atypically alluring, tough, brainy actress, but the movies have little place in current times for the sort of forceful, pitiliess persona Helgenberger projects at her best. Her finest big-screen performance to date was as a raw-boned working-class woman helped by Julia Roberts in *Erin Brockovich* (2000). That same year, she was perfect as Patsy Ramsey, the hard-shell, emotionally shell-shocked suburban mother in an otherwise standard exploitation-TV-movie, *Perfect Murder, Perfect Town: JonBenet and the City of Boulder*. Otherwise, she's been sidelined in schlock in feature films like *Bad Boys* and *Species I* and *II*.

No, it's on the small screen where Helgenberger radiates power and shrewdness. She won a Best Supporting Actress Emmy playing KC in *China Beach*, an overrated look at Vietnam, with Dana Delaney and Helgenberger transcending the *M*A*S*H*-as-a-drama gab-fest that William Broyles and John Sacret Young created with great, excessive earnestness. Watching any episode of *Beach* now, especially its maudlin final episode, one of those reunion shows where most of the characters paint snow-white streaks into their dark hair to convey age, KC remains a brassy redhead. Though portrayed by the script as a lonely woman who's incomplete for having abandoned her daughter during the '60s, KC is now—thanks to a clever plot idea and, even more, Helgenberger's performance—a wealthy businesswoman: a prostitute redeemed in the eyes of the boardroom, if not society.

Her Catherine Willows on *CSI* is fully the equal of star William Petersen in terms of ability and hardboiled impatience. In a better TV world, she, not Petersen, whose practiced stoicism tends toward the wooden, would be the leader of this Las Vegas crime unit. The distinctive, much-noted camera style of *CSI*—with its swooping dives into the bodies of corpses to explore wounds with microscopic intensity—also forces close-ups of the investigators' faces as they lean in close, flashlights in hand, to peer at death. The fine lines on Helgenberger's face tell Catherine's "back story" better than the few clues the series drops about her private life. Learning that the avuncular old Vegas coot who rescued her from stripping was actually her father and a murderer to boot may have startled Catherine initially, but she recovered quickly, sizing the situation up as one more way in which men screw over women in endless, myriad ways. This is Helgenberger's gift as a performer—to convey a scarred-over vulnerability that doesn't rely on TV's standard tropes of rote feminism or male-identified dependency. Sure, it's not likely that many real-life CSI forensic sleuths wear scoop-neck shirts, tight jeans, and high-heeled boots, but Helgenberger has spent her career pulling off unlikely getups and setups without actually removing any of her dignity.

Hate

John Larroquette: Dark Rider to No Place Special

Winner of four consecutive Emmy Awards for his supporting role as the arrogant, priapic Assistant District Attorney Dan Fielding in the unaccountably, only-in-the-'80s popular sitcom *Night Court*, Larroquette is probably a very nice man in real life. Or maybe not. In either case, he is representative of a certain kind of TV performer. He's smart enough to know that he does one thing well—in his case, smug knowingness—and should not bother trying to "branch out" and try anything new. At the same time, he fails to recognize that that same thing has become tiresome, and why should he? The industry encourages him to avoid what ought to happen (i.e., early, surely cushy retirement) and keeps giving him both work and awards. He was handed a 1998 guest-actor Emmy, for example, as a reward for playing psychotic killer Joey Heric in *The Practice*—essentially, of course, Dan Fielding as a murderous nutcase. Which is what some of us always thought Assistant D.A. Fielding always was anyway, when he went home alone in the wee hours of the morning after a night-court session.

Larroquette is certainly not without a small, carefully honed talent. No matter whom he's playing, he does a solid poker-face double-take and enunciates with comic precision. (In this, though, he is surpassed by Kelsey Grammer's Frasier Crane.) On *Night*

Court, as a supporting character to a nonactor—the "funny" one-time magician Harry Anderson—the six-foot-four Larroquette was a giant among thespian pygmies, even when placed next to a taller tiny-talent, the late Richard Moll (Bailiff Bull).

The cascade of Emmys—which probably would have continued had Larroquette, again, no dummy, not removed himself from contention after his fourth-in-a-row win—pushed Larroquette into TV-star status. His 1993–1996 series, *The John Larroquette Show,* had all the hallmarks of the middlebrow overreacher. Known from interviews to be an assiduous reader, he called his recovering-alcoholic bus-station night-manager character John Hemingway, an assiduous reader who, like, the actor himself, collected Thomas Pynchon first editions. CNN reported that the reclusive author once called the actor to "offer suggestions and corrections," thus proving that (a) no one is immune to TV's blandishments, and (b) Larroquette was not so assiduous that he was getting his Pynchon facts straight. TV Guide called the *Larroquette Show* a "sitcom noir," reason enough to avoid this alternately faux-downbeat, oddly pretentious little project. Hemingway kept a sign in his office, filched from an amusement park, that read, "This Is a Dark Ride"—we were supposed to be impressed that Larroquette was trafficking in gloom and irony in a sitcom context. It was, like most of Larroquette's work, at once clever and smirky. Cringe-inducing. A ride with a garrulous driver that makes you want to get out of the car and take your chances hitchhiking.

Love

Look What You Can Do with a Penknife:
The Pilot Episode of *MacGyver*: September 28, 1985

There are scads of shows you only need to watch once to extract the essence of their limited but undeniable pleasures. This is true of everything from overrated series ranging from *Moonlighting* to *Murphy Brown*. *MacGyver* is a perfect example of this. Watch the pilot and you've seen every episode. An agent for the Phoenix Foundation, a private organization that did secret missions for the government, Richard Dean Anderson's MacGyver, you'll recall, had a gimmick—he got himself out of jams using ordinary items like a Swiss Army knife or a book of matches. The rugged, thatched-haired MacGyver also wore layered clothes years before it was fashionable, thus making him far easier to watch than most '80s fashion victims.

In the premiere, one of the first greetings jack-of-all-emergencies "Mac" receives from a government superior is, "You must be the screwball," thus signalling, of course, not oddity at all, but a TV-easy rebellious streak and unorthodox manner. The Minneapolis-born Anderson dropped his "g"s and spoke in a folksy twang that suited his it's-all-good casual approach to getting himself out of life-threatening situations. "Watch yore step now," he'd say. "This is nasty stuff we're lookin' for." The pilot hour took care to set up the character, even having him explain the capacious knapsack he invariably carried: "The bag's not for what I take . . . it's for what I pick up along the way."

Like . . . chocolate bars. In that debut, MacGyver was called upon, to stop an acid leak that had caused an explosion in a nuclear-weapon substation—one that had trapped (get this) "two Nobel Prize nominees!" Accompanied for no good reason other than the hour needed a hotsy woman and a body to ask questions of, the curvy "scientist" asked how Mac expected to stop impending doom with a handful of candy bars he'd picked up in the rubble of the explosion.

"To you they're milk chocolate," said MacGyver in the first of countless spiels he would give over the course of the series, explaining his Idiot's Guide to the Universe philosophy. "But to sulphuric acid, it's lactose and sucrose, C12, H22 0-11: disaccharide; the acid will react with the sugar to form an elemental carbonate, a thick gummy residue—it should be enough to clog up that rupture." MacGyver paused and gave the girl a disarmingly modest grin. "Temporarily at least," he finished, delivering his greatest speech, a real mouthful.

MacGyver tapped into Reagan-era can-do resourcefulness; with his extensive knowledge of chemistry and physics, MacGyver was one of the few TV action heroes of whom it could be said was an educational influence—or at least a welcome throwback to boy's-book adventurism at a time when "boy's books" were becoming an unknown phrase to a generation weaned on *Brady Bunch* illiteracy. The character was a grown Boy Scout who didn't need high-tech gadgetry. MacGyver (no first name—at least, not until the series' final episode in 1992, when it was revealed to be "Angus") probably appealed to a professional nostalgist like *Happy Days*'s Henry Winkler, who was an executive producer. (Another producer was Vin DiBona, who went on to make fun of real people's thwarted resourcefulness in shows like *America's Funniest Home Videos*.)

Late in the series' inevitably sputtering run, Mac developed a cornball recurring archenemy called Murdoc played by former (if ever) rocker Michael Des Barres. Which reminds me of a trivia note: Anderson post-*Mac* performed with his own rock band, called Ricky Dean and Dante. He's since entered the purgatory of cult-TV stardom, but those initial sixty minutes of the pilot—which, by the way, are credited to "Alan Smithee," the long-time pseudonym for directors who want their name removed from a project of which they are ashamed—are pretty dang sweet. That Alan Smithee guy shoulda given himself some credit.

Hate

Home Makeover Shows: Where's the Wrecking Ball?

The Learning Channel has learned that there's no point in teachin' learnin' to folks—you gotta rev 'em up with cute carpenters, perky hostesses, and the vicarious dream/nightmare of having one's house redecorated as a flamboyantly garish mess! *Trading Spaces* quickly became TLC's most popular show with the premise of getting two sets of neighbors to exchange houses for forty-eight hours. With the help of the *Spaces* crew, a budget of $1,000, and more shortcuts than MacGyver could ever get away with, they turn one drab but livable room in each of their drab houses into a *colorful*, unlivable room. Paige Davis, the toothy host listed on the channel's Web site as "executive director in charge of making sure homeowners don't see what's happening in their room until the reveal on Day 2," gets each couple psyched for neighborly destruction/reconstruction. Meanwhile hunky, gelled-to-

the-max carpenter Ty Pennington and other professional home deco-
rators make the fantasies come true.

The entire series is, of course, a sham. In a typical episode set in a
sad little housing development in Skippack, Pennsylvania, for example, one couple reveals that they always wanted their bedroom to be
"a tropical getaway." Cut to Ty talking to the other couple, asking
what they think the first couple's bedroom should look like. "Um,
kind of an island hut retreat space," says the woman. Ty, eyes mock-
agog, gulps, "You're kidding! Did somebody tip you off?" Turns out
he was thinking the same thing! Well, we just saw the original couple
talking about their tropical getaway dream—gee, y'think they may
have mentioned it to their neighbors one day? Soon *violá*: a new
headboard that's not really new, it's just their old headboard "cov-
ered with twigs and sticks!"

The makeovers don't really offer much in the way of useful home
decoration or repair tips—the hard labor is filmed in that wacky
sped-up old-silent-film manner, so you can't see all the mistakes,
spills, annoyance, and frustration. When the owners return to their
made-over rooms for what the pros call "the reveal" (tellingly, a term
borrowed from magicians working to the climax of a trick), the civil-
ians' response is either: "Oh, my God!" or, among the more modest,
"Oh, my gosh!" I'd say 70 percent of the time this positively framed
yelled reaction is belied by what you can read in their eyes, which is
more like, "Holy crap, how am I going to live with/clean/dismantle
all these twigs/garish ceiling paint/stupid designs stencilled to the
walls?" The series includes the disclaimer, "Everyone on our show is
told upfront that there's a chance they won't like the final design of
the room. Each applicant signs a release acknowledging that the
show is not responsible for redecorating a room that isn't to the own-

er's taste." In other words, if you don't like your tropical paradise bedroom that looks like a cheap shrunken Vegas honeymoon suite, you're screwed. And as Paige says, "I don't hang around for the reveal"; that is, she doesn't want to be there when the suckers bewail their neighbors' poor—or at least different from their—taste.

Trading Spaces, along with the channel's cannibalizing series *While You Were Out,* is a spectacle of middle-class suburbia more depressing than the collected short stories of Johns Updike *and* Cheever. People are, in the *Trading Spaces* vision, possessed of so little imagination, yet so yearning for a change in their environment (as well as a desire to be on TV) that they will spend two days painting, hammering, and being ordered around by the shows' stars—i.e., glorified Home Depot employees. The hosts, by contrast, become mainstream stars, with Pennington moving up to network hosting, for example, on ABC's *Extreme Makeover: Home Edition.* The general attitude of the hosts, carpenters, and designers toward their subjects was revealed by Paige at the climax of the Skippack show: "Bring in the monkeys!" Paige chortled. At least some monkeys live in natural tropical getaways . . .

Love

Simon Cowell: Brit Twit as Wit Crit

Unlike the show that made him a sort of idol, the Brit pop label-owner, A&R-man, chesty, chain-smoking, snotty-bloke Simon Cowell is bracingly unsentimental, which in a U.S. context means cynical and (provide your own whining noise) *meeeean*. He's also possessed of a sense of humor, which in U.S. pop-music terms means he's snarky and sarcastic with casual articulateness. Americans view him as the villain of *American Idol* because he delivered something never seen on U.S. TV these days: blunt, detailed criticism. Thank heaven for Cowell—in the midst of a series he coproduces, one that celebrates excessive emotionalism and the flawless but mannered performances of classic rock and schlock, he exposes one of America's most exasperatingly traits: the refusal to understand that criticism, when delivered in a precise, vivid, witty manner, is both entertaining in itself and necessary as a corrective to decades of American schoolroom philosophy. This is the Dr. Spock–inspired philosophy that a young person must be made to feel special simply for trying even minimally hard to accomplish the simplest task.

Cowell, more of a sellout than his *American Idol* cojudge Randy Jackson, whose credentials as a producer are mediocre but in good middlebrow taste, and less of one than Paula Abdul, who never met a moron she couldn't praise with camera-hogging effusiveness, is a power in his homeland, where he helped launch *Idol's* prototype TV show, *Popstars*, and oversaw the career of the more-#1-hit-singles-than-the-Beatles bland-o boy-group Westlife, as well as the first British *Idol* winner, the Rick-Astley-with-a-thyroid-condition bland-o Will Young. On these shores, he achieved his one true bit of authentic creativity, delivering sharp, sometimes-lazily-phrased, sometimes-brilliant instant analyses of *Idol* contestants. As he has put it, "We're trying to show what show business is really like— illogical. Sexist. No matter how big you are, you're going to be criticized." Amen, brother.

Hate

American Idol: **Come Back to the Raft Ag'in, Clay, Honey**

The first edition of *American Idol* served as a wake-up call—it alerted us to a national emergency of which I had not previously been aware: An entire generation of young people has now grown up thinking that the closed-eyes-croon, the insincere melisma, the exaggerated gestural mannerisms and songs chosen for their bombast-content are the best ways to entertain America. The appalling thing is, this generation is apparently correct, to judge by the ratings success of this tedious, detestable series.

American Idol is an English import, where it is called *Pop Idol*. The Brits have always had a higher regard for/tolerance of middle-of-the-road song-belters, from Cliff Richard to Rick Astley, of whom punk-generation warbler Nick Lowe sang, "And do you remember Rick Astley?/He had a big fat hit, it was ghastly." In America, the rock-critical mandate for "authenticity"—the notion that a truly creative artist writes and performs his or her own material, no matter how average or technically "bad" his or her voice is (the example that disproves the rule most gloriously is Bob Dylan)—has been paramount since, paradoxically enough, the British invasion of the Beatles: the rock group that established the "we write our own songs" credo as a sign of artistry. This is, of course, a canard: Was Frank Sinatra any less talented than Dylan because he didn't write his material? Of course not. Was Elvis Presley, who wrote none of his biggest hits, less talented than Barry Manilow, who wrote nearly all of his? Of course not.

Slowly, surely—and I peg it to the rise of Whitney Houston in the '80s, with her superb voice but distracting, ostentatious leaps of register, drawn-out syllables, and excruciated facial expressions intended to signal how hard she was working to achieve her effects—we ended up with hideous stars like Christina Aguilera, all squinched eyes, fluttery hands, and taffy-pulled syllabics. Recognizing that America was now a safe haven for florid hacks, producer Simon Fuller brought the *Idol* franchise to the network owned by the schlockiest mogul, Ruper Murdoch, and Fox premiered *American Idol* in June 2002.

A throwback to both old-fashioned talent shows and Chuck Barris's humiliation fest *The Gong Show, Idol* on this side of the pond features a panel of three judges—record producer Randy Jackson (go ahead, name a hit he's worked on—I dare you), former cheerleader, dancer, and post-disco washout Paula Abdul, and talent-scout/producer Simon Cowell, the latter the only Brit in sight, hired to dispense the sort of blunt judgment that is common in his homeland but anathema to his Americans.

In England, the *Idol* hosts were a couple of genial chuckleheads who gave out a barrage of insincere yuks signalling that they were in on the foolishness of the entire enterprise; here, we got Brian Dunkleman, a bad stand-up comic who was dumped after the first season, a walking future-trivia answer; and Ryan Seacrest, a pretty-boy radio and afternoon talk-show host with a smile so wide it gives the phrase "ear to ear" sudden dangerousness: you really feel that if Seacrest grinned a half inch more, the top of his head would come undone and fall off.

The producers discovered that American audiences love to watch people not only embarrass themselves, but they also like to hear them verbally abused for being untalented. Granted, there's a certain pleasure to be taken from this when twentysomething egomaniacs strut out for an audition and bleat "Let's Stay Together" with idiotic confidence, but *Idol* stretches out these winnowing-down sessions for hours and hours—even seeing smuggies dispatched by Cowell becomes boring after the third week.

And who makes it through the narrow funnel of *Idol*-otry? In the first season, it was Kelly Clarkson, a big-voiced belter with no personality. In the second, even more popular season, the competition narrowed to skinny white Clay Aiken and big, black Ruben Studdard, a Huck Finn and Jim pairing who, though supposedly locked in heated battle, took every opportunity to hug and support each other as they stood on the vast raft of a stage. (Clay and Ruben would have made the literary critic Leslie Fielder say, "See? See? I told you so!") Studdard won, but, as is so often the case in America, it was the white man who actually sold more records once their solo albums were released. Studdard stuck with bearish R&B and feeble nods to hiphop, while Aiken trilled the sort of trite crap, his voice aquiver, that makes teen girls find him—well, not sexy so much as ingratiatingly harmless.

Translation for baby boomers: Clay Aiken is the Neil Sedaka for the current generation. Except he doesn't write or arrange songs as Sedaka could. No matter how many careers it launches or records it sells, *American Idol* is irrelevant to popular music—nothing new can ever emerge from it, because it holds as its ultimate values conformity and imitation. Everything is orderly in the *Idol* universe, even the extreme emotions the singers feign, even the humiliation the first-round, off-the-street contestants are put through. Everyone, from the producers to the victims, is in on the formula. The series' contentious third edition produced as its winner Fantasia Barrino, the most soulful, least mannered finalist to date, but as always in America, race matters: *Idol* message boards were alight with comments about her "big lips" and her unworthiness to be an Idol because she's a single mother. The only comfort to be taken from all this is that it's just a matter of time before the formula finally becomes as boring to the millions of *Idol* junkies as it is to those of us who've sobered up in the presence of this swill, which is narcotic whenever it's not insidious.

Love

The Best Mothers in TV History

One from each decade.

1950s: Donna Reed's Donna Stone in *The Donna Reed Show* (1958–1966)

You may say I'm fudging a little here, since the bulk of Reed's series aired during the first half of the '60s, but I disagree. Even before her show premiered in '58, Reed had established herself as a paragon of firm, imaginative, open-hearted motherhood, to say nothing of sexy wifeliness, playing opposite Jimmy Stewart in Frank Capra's *It's A Wonderful Life*. But Reed's wholesome Iowa farm-girl looks limited her feature-film career, despite the fact that she won a Best Supporting Oscar for her playing-against-type trollop in *From Here to Eternity*. Reed turned to television to find her true place in eternity, starring in a series that was produced in part by her real-life husband, Tony Owen. (This same setup is true of Elizabeth Montgomery, another willowy wife/mother of many a baby boomer's dreams. Add Lucy and Desi and their Desilu Productions, and you've got the basis for an interesting monograph on female-male power-partnerships in pre-feminist times.)

As the wife of Dr. Alex Stone, chiseled Carl Betz, and mother of two, Shelley Fabares, who parlayed her TV fame to record the fine hit single "Johnny Angel," and Paul Petersen, who grew up to be a shrill child-actor advocate, Reed was a fantasy of American motherhood in pearls, skirts, and high heels, and a bracingly sensible mom, utilizing a frown that projected fierce discipline as her kids grew into teens. While scoffers ridiculed the actress by dubbing it *Madonna Reed Show*, the rest of us understood that Donna Stone used that frown, her sunshine smile, and the wily intelligence that radiated from her gleaming eyes to guide the family down the path of sensible decisions, all without being humorless or cutesy. The engagement with the real world that Reed single-handedly injected into *The Donna Reed Show* emerged later in her personal life, when she protested the Vietnam War and the proliferation of nuclear weapons with an organization she founded, Another Mother for Peace.

1960s: Frances Bavier's Aunt Bee in *The Andy Griffith Show* (1960–1968)

Okay, she was obviously Opie's *aunt*, not mother, but Frances Bavier's Bee Taylor understood that maternal affection could be doled out in soothing words and freshly made pies. Aunt Bee may have dithered and deferred to her nephew, Griffith's widower-sheriff Andy Taylor, but there she maintained a firm role in the upbringing of Ron Howard's willful, tow-headed Opie. The genius of this gentle sitcom was the way its fantasy surface—placid life in the never-world of Mayberry, North Carolina—belied the realistic emotions roiling inside every character, including Gomer but excluding Goober, the series' jump-the-shark character. Aunt Bee was a plugged-in town gossip, a fussbudget who got her way yet sacrificed much of her own personal life to raising a child in her senior years. She is the very model of the sacrificing mother.

1970s: Esther Rolle's Florida Evans in *Good Times* (1974–1979)

And Aunt Bee's devotion is exceeded only by that of Esther Rolle's Florida Evans, the paradigmatic African-American inner-city matriarch of *Good Times*. Rolle, a skilled stage actress, must have taken this diciest of roles—a spin-off from her role in *Maude* yet a vehicle for its breakout star, Jimmie "J.J." "Dy-no-mite!" Walker—for the salary. Especially in the series first few seasons, Rolle and the equally adept John Amos as her husband, James, created vital portraits of black parents under stress from lower-middle-class want and external threats to family security. No sitcom was better able to transcend the inherent corniness of a "very special episode" about, say, the dangers of drugs than *Good Times*, largely thanks to Rolle's ability to switch from rapid-fire joke-deliverer to anguished mother.

1980s: Meredith Baxter-Birney's Elyse Keaton in *Family Ties* (1982–1989)

Baxter-Birney's Elyse was a former hippie turned Establishment tool—a suburban mom—along with her husband Steven, played by the blandly affable Michael Gross. The then-novel premise of *Family Ties* was these tie-dyed-in-the-wool liberals had given birth to a teen tyro of a Young Republican, played by Michael J. Fox. With her soft blue eyes and softer voice, it was easy to imagine Elyse as the granola girl she'd once been. Indeed, it was no small leap to picture her dreamier self dropping acid in a park somewhere: in a way, Baxter-Birney was the sitcom version of the stoned sketch-comedy character Leigh French played on *The Smothers Brothers Comedy Hour's* "Have a Little Tea with Goldie" segments. At the same time,

Baxter-Birney was also convincing as a woman struggling to locate the middle ground between the redefinition of parental roles among '60s-era breadwinners (Elyse was, many forget, an architect, a job she enjoyed and which was a constant source of inner conflict as motherhood engulfed her), while refusing to allow Fox's Alex and Justine Bateman's Mallory to be as freewheelingly anarchic as she had been. Again, like Esther Rolle, Baxter-Birney was originally cast as the lead character—indeed, Elyse and Steven were said to have been based on the early lives of creator Gary David Goldberg and his wife—but soon became overshadowed by the exploding popularity of her TV son. And again like Rolle, Baxter-Birney dealt with the realignment of the stars with maturity, often using her diminished status to subtle effect—or at least subtle by the standards of a laff-a-minute studio-audience sitcom. It was reported that Baxter-Birney chafed under her increasingly diminished role as *Ties* turned into *The Michael J. Fox Show*, to the point of trying to get out of her contract. But she was enough of a pro to conceal that contempt on-camera. Once she'd divested herself of husband-actor David Birney, Baxter became one of the better, more convincing regulars in the '80s roundelay of women-in-jeopardy TV movies, always a pleasure to watch for her steely reserve and the graceful beauty of her finely wrinkled middle age.

1990s: Kristine Sutherland's Joyce Summers in *Buffy the Vampire Slayer* (1997–2003)

This decade's most underrated mother—and who wouldn't be underrated playing a mortal parent, the only non-Scooby-gang regular in a supernatural cult smash?—was Kristine Sutherland's Joyce Summers. A single mother, Joyce strives even more mightily than most to understand a teenaged daughter who had a secret identity as nothing less than The Chosen One. If creator Joss Whedon's brilliant organizing metaphor was that high-school years are like doing battle with soul-depleting vampires and werewolves, his writing staff's constantly ingenious contribution was to avoid turning Joyce into a monster of repression or guilt. Joyce's mother-daughter colloquies with Sarah Michelle Gellar's Buffy possess a witty conversational shorthand and a realistic strain, as the parent yearns for the child to simultaneously confide in her and grow free of the necessity to do so. Whedon and company rewarded Sutherland for her valiant labor by giving her the greatest exit scene of any mother in television history. In the fifth-season episode entitled "The Body," Joyce dies of a brain aneurysm, and the hour moves back and forth within Buffy's consciousness, which include joyous imaginations of Joyce's recovery, only to return to the "reality" of Joyce's cold, dead body. As directed by Whedon, the episode, which contained no opening credits and no incidental music, emphasized the centrality of motherhood in even a life as otherworldly as that of a vampire slayer. To the end, Sutherland played Joyce as a serene woman, who knows on some level that she can never fully understand her daughter but treasures the aspects of her child that she does.

2000s: Lauren Graham's Lorelai Gilmore in *Gilmore Girls* (2000–present)

Too early to anoint a mother for the new millennium, but this creation of writer-producer Amy Sherman-Palladino will certainly be the one to beat. *Gilmore Girls* offers the mother-daughter relationship as an intense mutual understanding of love, loneliness, meals and secrets shared, jokes and pop-cultural references understood with minimal referents. If the show has a "message," it's that braininess trumps everything, with wit as its own glowing reward. Sherman-Palladino transcends the cliché of parent-as-best-friend by making sure that Lorelai advises, nudges, sets limits, and blows her stack at Alexis Bledel's Rory, but always returns to the idea that this mother—like Joyce Summers, a single parent—understands her job to be the issuance of a new, improved version of young female adulthood into the world.

Hate

The Worst Mothers in TV History

I shall choose one from each decade. The all-time worst mother is, of course, Florence Henderson's Carol Brady on The Brady Bunch, *but I give that series enough grief elsewhere.*

1950s: Barbara Billingsley's June Cleaver in
Leave It to Beaver (1957–1963)

As cold and hard as the pearls around her neck, June Cleaver was a mother/wife straight out of an early John Cheever short story: a creature of the most affluent suburbs, June was, on the surface, deferential to her husband (Hugh Beaumont's Ward) when it came to disciplining her sons Wally (Tony Dow) and Beaver (Jerry Mathers), but she used her role as subservient suburban helpmate to shape her sons' characters in her own way. This was primarily a matter of neglect: June led a busy social life, hosting coffee klatches and dinner parties. Boys were mainly creatures of dirt and mischief, to be cleaned and dispatched to their rooms as quickly as possible. When Ward, quick to criticize, would admonish Beaver and Wally for some infraction, June leapt to their defense and urged Ward not to be "too hard on the boys." However, when she greeted her husband at the end of his workday, June was the one who ratted out her sons, stroking Ward's ego and his anger, knowing that her secret will of dominance and control over her sprouting sons would be carried out by the leader of the clan. Was it any wonder that a 1983 TV movie, *Still the Beaver*, found the Beav divorced, overweight, and at loose ends—unable to cope with the adult world, because he'd been so persistently infantilized by Mom? In all this, it should be said, Billingsley gave a terrifically underplayed, chillingly precise performance.

1960s: Mary Tyler Moore's Laura Petrie in *The Dick Van Dyke Show* (1961–1866)

Yes, she looked fabulous in those capri pants. Yes, she would go on to become America's sweetheart in *The Mary Tyler Moore Show*. But in taking what the writers handed her on the *The Dick Van Dyke Show*, Moore was a weak-willed, indulgent mother to her sappy little boy Ritchie (Larry Matthews), all the more pernicious for being so beguiling to grown-ups. In a 1961 episode, "The Sick Boy and the Sitter," Laura doesn't want to go to a cocktail party, just because Ritchie has refused his daily afterschool cupcake. She thinks he's coming down with an illness. Dick warns Laura that she's being "oversolicitous and overprotective, and that can be bad for a mother," and he's right: Just look at the way Laura dressed Ritchie in the evenings—those pajamas, bathrobe, and pleather slippers are the stuff of future psychiatrist bills.

Speaking of doctors, the *Van Dyke Show* was very much of its era in the child-rearing department: Laura regularly invoked Dr. Spock, the high priest of permissive parenting. In another episode, "A Word A Day," in which Ritchie spouts a four-letter word without fully knowing its import, she tells Rob he's wrong to tell the little brat his salty tongue is unacceptable. "I say ignore it," says Laura with a prissy frown, or "he'll use it every time he wants to get attention." She never hears the advice proffered by Morey Amsterdam's Buddy: His father, he says, would have given him "a sharp chop in the mouth." I side with Buddy's dad. A stay-at-home mother (her dancing career thwarted by the traditions of the time period, an issue dealt with in other episodes), Laura ends up wanting to "keep evil away" from Ritchie—an alarmingly vehement reaction in a sitcom mom.

But Ritchie proves to be a whiner, a cajoler, the kind of kid who trades his baseball cards for a turtle so he can "make turtle soup"— he's one step away from taking a box of matches to a cat. He's eventually pushed to the margins of the series, until by the end of its run, he barely exists. Laura, while heaping guilt on her husband for missing so much as one of Ritchie's thoroughly mediocre school performances (we hear him butcher Cole Porter), is a thoroughly mediocre mother, more concerned with pleasing her man and nursing the grudge of giving up those sexy dancing tights than she is in raising a healthily obstreperous son. That kid should have been spanked more often, treated to some cowboy pajamas, and allowed to run around barefoot once in a while.

1970s: Jean Stapleton's Edith Bunker in *All in the Family* (1971–1980)

What can you say about a woman who continued to live with a venomous bigot like Archie Bunker and kept her daughter in his poisonous presence? Stapleton, who won three well-deserved Emmys for her heroic portrayal of Edith, is the ultimate TV battered wife: insulted, bullied, servile, and morose. Her perpetually downturned eyes and mouth say it all without a word. Edith suffered a rape, breast cancer, and, ultimately, death. As the seasons passed, Edith became a "stronger" character—she stood up to Archie more, the "Dingbat," Archie's belittling nickname for her, telling the monster to "stuff it."

That didn't help Sally Struthers's Gloria, a moon-faced girl with banana-curls and a wide smile. We can presume that until she met Michael "Meathead" Stivic (Rob Reiner), Gloria had no strong buffer from Archie's crippling verbal abuse. You can see in the early episodes of the series, from Struthers's hunched-shoulders, turned-in-toes posture, that this is a girl used to being berated or left looking for the nearest opportunity to escape to her bedroom, or outside to a world where Archie was able to be eluded. It certainly took all of Edith's strength just to keep Archie at bay from herself—she had neither the time nor the will to defend Gloria as well.

In later years, Gloria, encouraged and emboldened by boyfriend-turned-husband Mike, became a strident feminist, screeching her disagreement with Archie's vituperations. Yet Gloria's failure to have a nurturing relationship with either parent left her unable to build a solid union as an adult: Gloria and Mike divorced, something Edith should have done many years earlier—left the bellowing bastard together with her impressionable daughter before he damaged them both.

Every time I see Struthers now in those commercials as the grasping spokesperson for some poor-children charity no one I know ever donates money to, I think people can't see the images of starving kids; they're too busy saying, "*That's* Sally Struthers?" Ditto, same viewer question regarding her yammering-neighbor recurring role on *The Gilmore Girls*, which seems like the sort of charity work you'd give to Gloria Bunker when she hit her inevitably sad, lonely middle age. Shame on you, Edith, for letting it get this bad.

1980s: Susan Saint James's Kate and Jane Curtin's Allie in *Kate & Allie* (1984–1989)

Two thirtysomething divorcees with three children between them, Kate and Allie were presented as postfeminist role models when their series premiered, and the rare subsequent analysis of this popular but ultimately anonymous sitcom occasionally deduces that the pair could be viewed as an encoded lesbian couple with a blended family. Not a difficult conclusion to come to, actually, when you consider dialogue like this nugget, unearthed in Rick Mitz's useful *The Great TV Sitcom Book* (1988): Allie: "Kate do you want to get married again?" Kate: "Some day." Allie: "It wasn't a question; it was a proposal." Kate worked at a travel agency; Allie was the stay-at-home mom. And they lived in *Greenwich Village*, fer Pete's sake.

Well, whatever: Kate and Allie were lousy parents. Kind critics began referring to *Kate & Allie* as "the first feminist sitcom," but that was primarily because the show was nearly all about *them—their* problems, *their* unfulfilled desires, *their* emotional highs and lows. The kids, played by Ari Meyers, Frederick Koehler, and Allison Smith, might as well have been street urchins, for all the attention they got from Mom and Mom. And when they did, it was the sort of wry, talking-over-the-kids'-heads chatter that adults do when they're ostensibly aiming their remarks at their children but are really talking to their mates. By the end of the series' run, Kate and Allie were still inseparable, but had become insufferable. Allison Smith, I can note, went on to be a fine actress in the short-lived *Buddy Faro* and the movie *Holes*. Curtain did time on *Third Rock from the Sun*; Saint James married a TV exec known primarily for his brutish business tactics, Dick Ebersol, and seems in retirement at this writing. Does anyone watch *K&A* in its rare syndication or cable runs? No. Selfish feminism proved to be boring TV over the long haul.

1990s: Helen Hunt's Jamie Buchman in *Mad About You* (1992–1999)

Pity poor Mabel, the caterwauling plot device dragged into the sitcom world at the end of *Mad About You*'s fifth season to boost the show's sagging ratings. By 1997, audiences were getting a tad tired of the mutual self-absorption society that Jamie and Paul Reiser's Paul had created, and so they went for the oldest stunt in the book: they pulled an *I Love Lucy*, but devoted not one but two episodes to what they entitled "The Birth." Not until the start of season six was the baby girl brought home and finally named: Mabel, because its spelling, Jamie's mother said (file this under "The Apple Not Falling Far from the Tree Dept.") was a mnemonic device that stood for "Mothers Always Bring Extra Love."

Can you imagine being raised by a mother who would insist on inserting credit for herself in your own name? By this time, Hunt and Reiser were making so much dough, they seemed to have lost sense of how out-of-touch they were with their audience, so much so that I assume they thought this was the cutest idea imaginable. In keeping with the tone that had seeped into this once-charming sitcom, the first full season of Mabel-plots only proved what a tiresomely selfish person Jamie was, encouraged in her behavior at every step by Paul.

We got half-hours built around Jamie, writing a letter to Mabel to be read on the kid's eighteenth birthday, at which time the girl's resentment and rebelliousness would have built to such an extent she'd probably be in a Buddhist monastery, deprived of worldly goods like birthday letters. There was the famous-among-dwindling-fans "real-time" episode in which Jamie and Paul, in order to put Mabel on a sleep schedule, let her cry virtually all night. As usual, everything was about Jamie's exhaustion, with the baby already a nuisance. There was the postpartum depression episode, in which Jamie vents about her pregnancy weight and being seen by the outside world: "I am having a hair problem. I'm having a clothing problem, because suddenly I'm shaped like a Dr. Seuss character. So I'm not dying to be seen in public right now!"

Mad About You ultimately slipped into the obscurity of solipsism, but whenever I come across the title of the show, I worry about Mabel, and whether she'll ever have a female figure in her life she can feel loves her unconditionally—or even just without conditioner in her hair.

Love

The Best Fathers in TV History

One from each decade.

1950s: Frank Faylen's Herbert T. Gillis in *The Many Loves of Dobie Gillis* (1959–1963)

Just under the decade-wire, here was a father who, unlike some smug suburban businessman-dads we knew, really *did* know best. Frank Faylen's Herbert was a humble grocery-store owner, dad to Dobie (Dwayne Hickman), a proto-playa with the ladies—and whatta lady: Tuesday Weld's tight-sweatered Thalia Meninger—a generally mediocre student and a lazy adolescent. Herbert took his role as parent seriously. He made Dobie work in the grocery store, stacking cans while dreaming of Thalia's. He grounded the kid when he needed punishment, and yelled at the little smirking punk when he needed to be taken down a peg or two. Herbert T. Gillis—his use of his middle initial signalled poignantly his yearning for upper-middle-class respectability—was a fine, aggressively nonpermissive parent in an era in which foundations were cracking. Bob Denver's beatnik Maynard G. Krebs, with his labor-avoiding catchphrase "Work? *Work!*"—i.e., What, *me? Work?*—was, Herbert recognized, a poor influence on his son. If the poor slump-shouldered bastard had seen the '60s counterculture coming, he would have chased Dobie around the store, hitting his progeny with his broom, much more often. Hardworking fathers all over the country should salute the underrated Mr. Gillis.

1960s: Fred MacMurray as Steve Douglas in *My Three Sons* (1960–1972)

MacMurray, who'd made his most indelible impression in the movies as the hardboiled insurance con-man/romantic sucker in *Double Indemnity* (1944) had, by the late '50s, moved into the downward trajectory of Disney movies, playing a befuddled dad in 1959's *The Shaggy Dog*, regained some degree of dignity and provided a fine masculine role model in *My Three Sons*. A widower father, aeronautical engineer Steve Douglas raised his trio of spunky sons first with the aid of his no-nonsense father-in-law, Bub, *I Love Lucy*'s William Frawley. When Frawley left the series due to illness in '65, the kids' Uncle Charley, played by William Demarest—doing a toned-down but still effectively grumpy variation on his finest big-screen moment, in Preston Sturges's *The Miracle of Morgan's Creek*—took over. Some critics have written that MacMurray seemed to spend more time at home than he did at work, but this doesn't allow for the elastic sense of time in sitcoms, nor the fact that Steve was often shown bringing his work home, nor the fact that MacMurray played this character just right.

He cultivated an air of being approachable yet always a little preoccupied. He was there for his sons, who could get his attention with a little effort—"Hey, Dad, Chip's turtle is lost!"—but he was also a dreamy, imaginative sort, a creative man yet not an artist; a businessman yet not a deskbound drone. It's said that MacMurray didn't think much of the role—which was, after all, just pleasant piffle, with punchlines written to provoke muted chuckles, not thigh-slapping. He arranged to have all his scenes filmed over a few days in the work week. In his useful book *Honey, I'm Home!* (1992), author Gerard Jones quotes MacMurray as saying that working on *Sons* was "like working long weekends, that's all." The result wasn't a half-hearted performance; MacMurray managed to convey genuine curiosity about the boys' activities and school and social challenges. MacMurray had a natural diffidence about him that perfectly suited the open-minded, trusting father Steve Douglas was.

1970s: Redd Foxx as Fred Sanford in *Sanford and Son* (1972–1977)

Some might say cantankerous junkyard-owner Fred Sanford belongs on a worst-father list, since his dialogues with his adult son Lamont (Demond Wilson) were primarily litanies of complaint, pessimism, and distrust of the world. As a black man who'd survived the white world well into his sixties—during some of the most tumultuous times in civil rights and changing attitudes toward blacks—Fred is a battered, teetering, but still-standing tower of survival.

Foxx, a veteran nightclub comic well-known to black audiences for his bestselling, X-rated "party records," brought a lot of his own anger to Fred's character. Although white liberals in the media fretted that Fred was a reverse–Archie Bunker, making disparaging remarks about whites and Asians, black viewers (among others—*Sanford* was a big, across-the-demographics hit) appreciated Fred's sense of freedom. He might be a junk-dealer, but he was his own boss; he took guff from no one. When a white police officer asked Fred, who had reported a robbery, if he thought the perpetrators were "colored,"

Foxx fixed him with the cold, hard stare he gave nightclub audiences just before delivering the punchline blow. "Yeah . . . *white!*," he rumbled. *Sanford and Son* also served as a showcase for a generation of black comic actors who'd been invisible to mainstream audiences including LaWanda Page as mouthy Aunt Esther, Slappy White as the genial Melvin, Beah Richards as kindly Aunt Ethel, and Whitman Mayo, who, as the thoughtfully deliberate, methodical Grady Wilson, got his own spin-off show, a four-month flop. Just as Dobie's dad Herbert was determined to tell his son of the hard realities of life, so did Fred Sanford prod and provoke Lamont into being a good son who'd make something of himself.

1980s: John Goodman as Dan Connor in *Roseanne* (1988–1997)

If it was the title star who made the most noise and grabbed all the media attention, it was Goodman, along with costar Laurie Metcalf as his sister-in-law, Jackie, who provided the professional performance that helped *Roseanne* become the finest portrait of white working-class life in TV history, until it went wacko-surreal in the final two seasons. Goodman's Dan Connor was an honest laborer, a contractor and mechanic, who was occasionally out of work and who later ran a motorcycle shop. Goodman's girth helped give Dan literal and dramatic heft. It was easy to believe that this big guy could do heavy lifting, raise little hellions, go toe-to-toe with a bellicose spouse, and still take comfort in the evening with a few beers and a warm TV.

As a pro with a budding movie career, it must have been difficult for Goodman to withstand the gifted but neurotic Roseanne's adjustment to stardom, but he never complained to the press. This centeredness came through in his role as father, whether dealing with his three kids, particularly the moody Darlene (Sara Gilbert), teasing smiles out of her with gentle joshing, comforting her when she cuts her finger by telling her to "think about a pretty flower"—a touching leap of banal imagination for a blue-collar hero. If Dan would go to some lengths to avoid fixing a clogged sink or toilet, he never let down his family—and when he did, by, say, getting low-balled on a contracting-job bid, he always kept up appearances, such as his were, kidding the kids about their young romances or fights with friends. I always noted that Dan knew the names of his kids' friends, an infallible sign of a good father, I have noticed in real life. He'd waggle his enormous fanny as he bent over into the 'fridge, looking for that last beer, knowing that it was best to take comfort in the small amusements of life to achieve larger happiness.

1990s: Billy Campbell's Rick Sammler in *Once & Again* (1999–2002)

The divorced dad gets a bad rap in most TV shows—he's the guy who comes in and out of his kids' lives, sometimes giving financial and emotional child-support, as often as not, not. He's a womanizer or just a spineless creep. Not Campbell's Rick, a smart, sensitive architect struggling with why his marriage with high-strung control freak Karen (the magnificent Susanna Thompson) went wrong and worried about how the new love of his life (hel-*LOOO*, Sela Ward!) will affect his children, the sensitive (this was a *thirtysomething*-producers show, so from here on out it goes without saying that *everyone* was sensitive) brooder Eli (Shane West) and his fragile middle daughter Jesse (luminous Evan Rachel Wood).

Campbell, whose previous chief starring role had been in a re-sounding flop, the 1991 superhero vehicle *The Rocketeer*, used his multitalented chin—chiseled *and* dimpled!—to prove it could be glass. Rick took life's punches hard. Yet to his and the writers' credit, he was no wimp. He marshalled his strength and will to cope with the realistically maddening divorce details of which kid is spending what weekend with which parents and stood up for his more laid-back parenting style against Karen's dictatorial approach. *Once & Again* limped along in the ratings for two seasons, but Campbell came through it all with the lopsided dignity of a guy who's got to put a work deadline on the back-burner in order to have pizza and homework-time with his progeny. He did that rare thing—he made divorced dads proud.

Hate

The Worst Fathers in TV History

I shall choose one from each decade. The all-time worst father is, of course, Robert Reed's Mike Brady on The Brady Bunch, *but I give that series enough grief elsewhere.*

1950s: Danny Thomas's Danny Williams in *The Danny Thomas Show* (1953–1971)

He was just so *loud*, so quick to yell, so frightening to me as a child, and I don't think I'm projecting *too* much—cough-cough—to his

TV son, the perennially startled-looking little Rusty Hamer. Thomas always fascinated me: He was Lebanese—what the heck was that, I wondered as a kid? He'd often tap his nose, the size of a macaw's bill, when boasting about his heritage or his outsize wisdom and he had an Uncle Tonoose who was in part convincingly cast because of his own long proboscis. (I later learned Uncle Tonoose was the great Hans Conreid, whose *least* accomplishments were the marvelously purred narrations he did for *Rocky and Bullwinkle*'s "Fractured Fairy Tales.") Playing Danny Williams, a barely fictionalized version of the yammering song-and-dance man Thomas was himself, I'd noticed the star had fascinating hands as well. His index fingers, in repose, remained pointed almost straight out, while the rest of his fingers bent in an ever-decreasing curl, until the pinky was wound tight. They were hands that had never performed manual labor, hands made to open up and be held aloft during the climax of a song, hands in the shape of seashells.

But Danny Williams was a lousy father. The same characteristics that made him believable as a nightclub star—an aggressive, knock-'em-dead attack meant to be heard over the clink of scotch-and-soda glasses—clearly scarred not only his put-upon wife, the stunning, innocently sexy Marjorie Lord, who'd replaced the harder-looking Jean Hagen in the '56 season, but also Howard's Rusty and Angela Cartwright's doll-like Linda. In their posh Manhattan apartment, Danny's barked commands and howled indignation sometimes literally paralyzed the family. When they froze in the wake of one of his icy blasts of rage/confusion/triumph, they didn't seem to be acting. When you watch a show and part of you is wondering whether the star screams as much at the kids off-camera as he does on, you know you have a father-figure who's a kind of monster of ego and id.

1960s: Bill Bixby's Tom Corbett in *The Courtship of Eddie's Father* (1969–1972)

Tom Corbett was praised for his laid-back, adult-hippie approach to fatherhood at a time when it was perceived as a good, progressive thing to make your kid your *friend* (the series theme song was, after all, Harry Nilsson's lovely "Best Friend"). Corbett was the worst kind of narcissist: a dashing widower who let his son (scrunched-face cute Brandon Cruz) set him up with honeys—the son in hopes of getting a new mom; Dad in the hope of getting laid. It must have been like having the young Warren Beatty as your father.

1970s: Carroll O'Connor's Archie Bunker in *All in the Family* (1971–1983)

A too-easy call, you say? Pish-tosh: Remember that, for all his intemperate ranting, racism, and wife-abuse, Archie became a beloved figure in American pop culture, a symbol of the white working-class male marginalized by the counterculture, feminism, liberal social policy, and emergent political correctness. Archie's Queens, New York, throne—his tattered centerstage living-room chair—is enshrined in the Smithsonian.

Much has been written about Jean Stapleton's Edith, and the way she slowly, steadily outwitted and stood up to Archie, but the permanently damaged figure in this *Family* was the Bunkers' only child, Sally Struthers's Gloria. Where her boyfriend-then-husband,

Michael "Meathead" Stivic (Rob Reiner) was permitted to get in Archie's face, Gloria, in the series' early years, did little more than whine, yelp, submit to Archie's strictures, run to Edith for support she rarely received, and stood literally behind Michael in many a family battle. In later seasons Gloria became a jargon-spouting feminist, but her rhetoric never matched her defeated, fearful, sad-sack demeanor.

When Struthers appeared in Sam Peckinpah's 1972 Steve McQueen–Ali McGraw thriller *The Getaway*, she played her small role as a Gloria gone bad, a Gloria who'd given up. In the movie, the husband of Struthers's character is taken hostage, and she quickly sides with his captors, humiliating hubby by having sex with the thugs. This would have been Gloria's ultimate revenge against Archie, a dad who deserved to have Social Services come to his famous stage-right front door and have his only offspring removed from his tyrannical custody.

1980s: Ken Olin's Michael Steadman in *thirtysomething* (1987–1991)

Intent on launching a career as a Philadelphia ad-man, Michael Steadman was an '80s version of a typical male protagonist in a Richard Yates novel: depressed, driven, put-upon, invariably left feeling misunderstood. A yuppie with soulful eyes mainly for his Modiglianiesque wife Hope, played by Mel Harris, Michael had scant time for their infant daughter Janey beyond numerous scenes of him looking at the newborn with wondering eyes. The camera was invariably placed, by creators Ed Zwick and Marshall Herskowitz, on Olin's gaze—he, not the child, was the true wonder, positioned as a devoted parent who was consumed with the bad idea of commencing parenthood just as he was also launching his own ad agency with his pal Elliott (Tim Busfield), another crappy dad who eventually left his wife, Patricia Wettig—Olin's real-life spouse— and his kids because of a roving eye as well as overweening ambition.

1990s: Ray Romano's Ray Barone in *Everybody Loves Raymond* (1996–present)

Not only one of the most popular sitcoms of the decade, one of the few popular ones at all to feature a family and a studio audience at the end of the '90s, *Everybody Loves Raymond* began its existence mining variations on the family-centric stand-up routines of comedian Romano as well as that of producer/co-creator Phil Rosenthal, himself once a less successful stand-up. The first two seasons or so were fun, with Ray Barone, a sportswriter working mostly from home, doing his best to shirk parental responsibilities to his young daughter and two younger twin boys, but the shirking was done in comic rhythm to costar Patricia Heaton, whose Debra was the long-suffering wife who refused to suffer. She forced Ray, still a spoiled son himself tied to the long apron strings of his nearby mother, TV vet Doris Roberts, to accept adult responsibilities that included a full-partnership parenthood.

But along about the third season, things turned sour. Heaton started playing Debra like a squalling harridan, increasingly bitter. And Ray Barone became nearly obsessed with an extramarital privacy—watching TV sports with his oaf brother Robert (Brad Garrett) and gargoyle father (Peter Boyle), or sneaking off to games with various buddies. The children, whom Romano and Rosenthal had, to give them proper credit, always were meant to be background noise to the Ray/Debra/Ray's-parents triangle.

Even in this context, Ray Barone became a dreadful father, uninterested in his kids unless they could bring him some residual glory, possessed of no patience for their barely articulated needs. A Clinton-era dad, Barone became a shirker, a prevaricator, a resentful baby boomer who was disinclined to love his babies while nurturing his own insatiable, infantile desires—sex, snack food, sports, and silence.

Love

The Tao of the Sitcom: *The Honeymooners* and *The Andy Griffith Show* as the Yin and Yang of a Genre

Two of the most nuanced sitcoms ever are at stylistic, philosophical extremes. *The Honeymooners*'s comic energy derives from its being urban, loud, and violently emotional; *The Andy Griffith Show* is pastoral, calm, and soothingly reassuring.

Jackie Gleason developed *The Honeymooners* from a series of skits he'd performed on an earlier variety opus, *The Jackie Gleason Show*. He conceived of a '50s twist—a kitchen-sink comedy in the era of the kitchen-sink drama—and flanked himself with two crucial characters, his loving but hardbitten wife (Audrey Meadows) and his faithful but stupid best friend (Art Carney). Given Gleason's resistance to rehearsing, it can't be said that he selflessly let his costars shine out of the goodness of his heart. It may be that Carney had the time to develop his elegantly dopey Ed Norton while waiting for the star to show up. However it happened, *The Honeymooners* remains endlessly watchable, its plots elementally simple—usually some get-rich-quick scheme Gleason's bus driver Ralph dreams up goes awry—and the camera, placed most often as though filming a play, pointed straight at the Kramdens' bare-bones kitchen, lets us watch instinctive acting and inspired improvisation, miraculously captured on tape.

By contrast, *The Andy Griffith Show* came from the wily urban mind of producer-actor Sheldon Leonard, who must have dreamed up the Southern town of Mayberry as a city-slicker's idea of heaven. Taking the folksy persona Griffith had worked out onstage, where he was more storyteller than stand-up comic, the series followed the tall, grinning star as a father and authority figure not only to his son Opie (Ron Howard) but to the entire town. Everyone, from Aunt Bee (Frances Bavier) to gas-pumper Gomer Pyle (Jim Nabors) idolized Sheriff Andy for his drawled wisdom and chuckling common sense. The *Griffith Show*, like *The Honeymooners*, was blessed with a terrific idiot man-boy costar: Don Knotts as nervous deputy Barney Fife.

Taken together, *The Honeymooners* and *The Andy Griffith Show*—one an urban nightmare-turned-moody-lullabye, the other a whistled nursery-rhyme idyll—define the opposite, most blissful extremes of the situations of sitcoms.

Hate

The Sensitive Cop: *Barney Miller*

Some shows are so dreadfully overrated as to merit special scrutiny. What is it about *Barney Miller* that burnishes its luster as a fondly remembered sitcom with a great ensemble cast? I believe it has primarily to do with the era in which it aired. *Miller* (1975–1982) preceded *Hill Street Blues* (1981–1987) as a "realistic" look at police work. It dared to be dull, mundane, depressing. More than one writer has compared *Barney Miller* to a comic version of Ed McBain's 87th Precinct novels, and that's apt—both feature unbelievable, stylized dialogue, predictable actions, and ethnic supporting players. I dare anyone to look at a *Miller* episode and tell me that this show was realistic.

Arrayed across a determinedly dingy stage set that passed for New York's 12th precinct—I'd be very surprised if the set designer hadn't seen William Wyler's 1951 policer *Detective Story*—*Miller* starred song-and-dance-man Hal Linden as the patient, intelligent, enlightened police captain, a character that had much in common, from temperament to rank, to Daniel J. Travanti's Frank Furillo on *Hill Street*. He presided over a carefully assembled array of ethnic stereotypes, from the big-pimpin' black police detective Ron Harris portrayed to the walking Polish joke Max Gail embodied as Det. Stanley "Wojo" Wojohowicz, from the strutting Puerto Rican cop played by Gregory Sierra to the unreadably blank-faced Asian played by the adroit Jack Soo. At a time when TV was less about youth demos and more about representing diversity, there was even a token old guy, Abe Vigoda's Fish. Early episodes included a female cop played by Linda Lavin well before her movie career and the sitcom *Alice*, but the male writers and producers had no idea what to do with either her or Barney's wife, played by the witty stage actress Barbara Barrie, and they were gone by the series' second season. *Barney Miller* was a deeply male, even sexist show. Constant, casually cruel jokes were had at the expense of gays and transvestites who were brought in as crime suspects.

The prevailing notion of much late-'70s television with aspirations to art, which cocreator Theodore "Ted" Flicker had in spades, as his crude but ambitious 1967 counterculture satire, the feature film, *The President's Analyst*, attests, was that verisimilitude could be brought to the small screen by actorly underplaying. I suppose that accounts for the overwhelming fan fondness for Fish, Vigoda's deadpan—rather, *corpse*-pan detective. Raising serious issues no matter whether or not a position is actually taken on said issue (such as a first-season episode in which the department is accused of taking graft), the final "artistic" touch involved regularly ending a scene of precinct noise and chaos on a deliberately quiet, faux-poignant note. The show had a perverse streak that was sometimes in stunning bad taste: In the '75 episode called "Snow Job," about a cold day without heat in the squad room, a flasher allowed out of the holding cell to use the men's room electrocutes himself off-camera. We're told he did it by holding on to a frozen pipe and a lightbulb socket. After the faux-poignance, a few more jokes are made at the man's expense regarding his flashing fetish.

Barney Miller really was McBain crossed with *Car 54, Where Are You?*, the latter an infinitely superior sitcom. What Miller's writers were aiming for was the TV equivalent of one of Donald Westlake's tough-minded and unsentimental comic crime novels. What they achieved, however, was pulp fiction of the sappiest, most sour sort.

Love

The Mona Lisa of Television: David Duchovny

He's the Princeton and Yale English-lit grad whose most famous character once described America as being run by the "military-industrial-entertainment complex." He's the actor portraying himself on Garry Shandling's *Larry Sanders Show* as a preening narcissist who finds Sanders's own preening narcissist irresistible to flirt with. He's the star who launched a gazillion Web sites, yet who once described his job to me as "pretty workaday . . . You get up, you take a shower, you read the paper, you play Mulder." He said this, as he says almost everything, on-screen and off-, with that enigmatic small smile, an anti-grin, an acknowledgment of the amusement of life, even if he doesn't quite share in the laugh.

David Duchovny is often described as being "deadpan," especially in the early days of the show that made him famous, *The X-Files*, but that's not true at all. He's more like an imp with restraint, a quality that served him well even before he entered the *X-Files* maelstrom of cult followings and inscrutable scripts. The title of his Ph.D. thesis was "Magic and Technology in Contemporary Poetry and Prose." His somber speaking voice was perfect for his first notable job, that of narrator for the Showtime network's soft-core cable-porno *Red Shoe Diaries*. No one could listen to Duchovny's diffident voiceovers and doubt that here was a gentleman who would one day portray a guy named "Fox" whose bachelor pad was a mess littered with some of the more hardcore stuff.

Duchovny's barely animated affect was perfect for *The X-Files*, a show that was often compared to everything from *The Twilight Zone* to *Twin Peaks*, in which, no coincidence, Duchovny played a role—that of a cross-dressing DEA agent. Creator Chris Carter declared he was inspired by the old '70s Darren McGavin show *Kolchak: The Night Stalker*, tales of the supernatural told by writer Richard Matheson with genuine jolts as well as an overlay of quiet, knowing humor. In the first season, you could see that Duchovny's costar, the less-experienced Gillian Anderson, was unsure of how to play Dana Scully from scene to scene. Sometimes she was too hard-boiled, sometimes too laid-back, other times verging on despair. But Duchovny had it nailed right from the start. He just met every smug FBI superior, every alien manifestation, with the same shadow of a smile, as if to say, "You think I'm a schmuck, but some day you'll come around to *my* way of thinking, schmuck." As he once remarked to me about *Files*, "If we ever revealed the secrets behind all this, the show would be unmasked as the ridiculous little hoax it is."

The Mona Lisa smile hasn't served him as well in movies. In the flimsy thriller *Kalifornia* (1993), it came off smug. In the charming romantic comedy *Return to Me* (2000) he seemed perpetually bemused—not a bad thing to be in a screwball comedy, but his face needed to register as much energy as Bonnie Hunt's script and directing demanded. There was a part of Duchovny that he withheld from the audience—the Princeton part, maybe, or the guy who was leery of committing lest he look like a sap.

TV remains Duchovny's medium. He was achingly funny on his three *Sanders* appearances. In the *Red Shoe/Twin Peaks* tradition, perhaps he's more free with his emotions when he's playing sexually upfront guys, even when that guy is a cartoon of himself, than when he's portraying a more conventional leading-man. The few episodes that Duchovny directed for *X-Files*, particularly the sixth-season baseball fantasy, "The Unnatural," were smooth and assured, yet brimming with emotion just beneath their surfaces. His direction was imbued with the same unknowable smile he brought to Fox Mulder's barren, obsessed life, making it glow as mightily as any hovering spacecraft. This slightly hidden quality in Duchovny, whether in front or behind the camera, may prove his long-term strength.

Hate

Six Feet Under: Alan Ball Buries *American Beauty*

If *The X-Files* dealt with the otherworldly, the stuff not of this Earth, ascending to the stars, *Six Feet Under* took the plunge, burrowing underground—or as underground as a gravedigger gets, which isn't very far. This superficial wound in the planet, inflicted to inter the dead, is in keeping with writer-creator Alan Ball's style, which is to get under your skin. He wants to disturb you, but not so much that you look away. So it was with his Oscar-winning script for *American Beauty*, which freed him from a career that had been spent churning out scripts for soul-crunching sitcoms like Cybill Shepherd's *Cybill* and Brett Butler's *Grace Under Fire*, and so it is with his extravagant, it's-not-TV-it's-HBO drama *Six Feet Under*.

The saga of the Fisher family of undertakers got off to a promising start in 2001, with an unshaven, morose Peter Krause—looking as though he'd just come off a bender after hearing of the cancellation of his piquant but pitifully rated sitcom *SportsNight*—wandering back home after years away. His father, the head of the mortuary, had just died, and Krause's Nate was there to pay his minimal respects and get the hell out, but he was pulled in, like the TV audience was. The family of miserable misfits—Nate's ditheringly weepy mother, Ruth (Frances Conroy), the anguished gay younger brother David (Michael C. Hall) bitter that Nate had left him holding the family (body-)bag years before, and the arty, moody teen sister Claire (Lauren Ambrose)—was needy in a way that was inescapable. Nate stayed on, and so did we. Soon he'd launched into a promising affair with a wild, bristlingly intelligent woman, Rachel Griffiths's Brenda, and had learned how to embalm a body from David. This, combined with vividly imagined regular visits from dead Dad (a wonderfully jaundiced Richard Jenkins), gave the series a combination of depression and uplift that seemed fresh as pushed-up daisies.

But then *Six Feet Under* had to go and win a lot of Emmys, and a complacent rot set in. By the start of the fourth season, Ambrose's Claire moans, "I'm sick of everything being so fucking awful all the time," and I was inclined to agree. A formaldehyde fog had settled over *Under*—it enveloped you with a serenity that used to be unsettling but now seems more like smothering. The show had become airless in its artful coolness and as formulaic as the sitcoms Ball had escaped. Every episode had to begin with a death scene, a client for the Fishers; each family member's individual emotional crisis was updated with assiduous regularity.

The same themes began to be repeated—Mother's lovers turned out to be creeps, one after another; David's boyfriend Keith (Matthew St. Patrick) went in and out of the closet with each new job he took; Krause suffered, suffered, suffered—Brenda went wonky and broke up with him, he married Lili Taylor's Lisa, but she got croaked. What began as a startlingly blunt look at death and its aftermath became lifeless and bleak. This left an exceedingly talented cast—especially Krause, Griffiths, and St. Patrick—standing around, as if contemplating their own demises. Or a network series, whichever opportunity arose first.

Love

The Subtle Torture of Adolescence: *Freaks and Geeks*

One of the most emotionally complex television series ever to package itself as a comedy, *Freaks and Geeks* lasted a pitifully short time—one season, eighteen episodes, 1999–2000. The show was set in the '80s and powered by the suburban hits of the period, Journey, Styx, Rush. It centered around the Weir family, in particular fifteen-year-old Sam (John Francis Daley) and seventeen-year-old Lindsay (Linda Cardellini). Sam was a runty geek, the kind of sensitive-faced lad who dreaded the day the gym teacher began enforcing showers, because he was ashamed of his scrawny, hairless body. Lindsay was a geek-turned-freak. In the space of a few remarkably written episodes, she went from being a straight-A, conscientious student—she was even part of the dorky "Mathletes" team—to becoming aware that life among her more rebellious classmates, the so-called freaks, had an irresistible allure. Putting away childish things, Lindsay starts wearing a big, shapeless, pea-green Army jacket and starts the noble adolescent task of Questioning Authority.

Except that on *Freaks and Geeks*, created by Paul Feig and his writer-producers, who included Judd Apatow (*The Cable Guy, The Larry Sanders Show*) and Mike White (*Chuck and Buck*), this trite TV and movie trope really *means* something. We see the price Lindsay pays for her rebellion: worry and hostility from parents and teachers, the loss of old geek friends, suspicion and hostility from the new gang she tries running with. We also get vividly detailed portraits of secondary characters whom most TV shows would just deploy for comic relief. The most poignant is Nick, a slack-jawed Jason Segel, who dreams of being a rock-star drummer but who must confront the fact that he's a merely mediocre musician surrounded by loser friends and, worse, a military-vet father. A perfect role for TV perennial tough-guy Kevin Tighe, the father threatens Nick that he's going into the Army if he doesn't maintain a C+ average, a hopeless goal for this sweet-tempered but rage-suppressing time bomb of a teen.

Sam's friends are similarly precisely drawn people, "types" who are rarely fleshed out beyond cartoon characteristics. Stocky little Neal (Samm Levine) is the Jewish kid who can imitate any sitcom shtick, who studies stand-up comics for their timing and analyzes humor with preternatural intensity. On Halloween, he goes out as Groucho Marx, and no one knows who he is. In the lunchroom, he asks his buddies with grave severity, "Did you see *Dukes of Hazzard* last night? Boss Hogg is *verrry* funny . . ." By contrast, Martin Starr's Bill Haverchuck is the gawky, bespectacled, impossibly long string-bean, who takes life's problems literally and expresses his thoughts with no id-filter. When Neal finds out his dad is having an affair, Bill blurts out, truly baffled, "I can't even get one girl. How do you get two?"

The Weir household was headed up by *SCTV* alum Joe Flaherty, who had grumpy, catastrophizing rage down better than a generation of mean ol' TV dads. When Lindsay displays a mild act of rebellion by having the hoody Daniel, played by the James Dean-ly James Franco, over to her house, Flaherty's Harold explodes, "Next thing you know she'll be Patty Hearst! She'll have a gun to our heads!" References to Hearst and arena rockers Rush sailed over the heads of too many viewers. *Freaks and Geeks*—as poignant every week as it was funny—never found a mass audience, but its out-of-nowhere quality remains alive in its DVD incarnation, thank the god of entertainment economics, wherein TV-freak-collectors benefit from geek-created technology.

Hate

The Price Is Right: The Public Is Wrong

A garish game show whose primary audience seems to consist largely of hungover college students who watch it instead of attending class, *The Price Is Right* requires no skill other than rudimentary addition and a ballpark idea of what a loveseat goes for at Wal-Mart. The patented competitions are like games of chance that probably make carnival workers snicker, sucker-bets designed for people who think Vegas slots are arm-pulls to fortune.

Some think Monty Hall's *Let's Make a Deal* was worse, a show that encouraged idiotic self-abasement by having audience members dress up as anything from chickens to bumblebees to get the host's attention. Its signature gimmick—guessing the most valuable prize hidden behind three doors—is all the more depressing for having been inspired by a mediocre literary work, O. Henry's "The Lady and the Tiger."

Price, which premiered in 1956 and is TV's longest-running game show, is worse for its sheen of respectability, its refusal to admit that it's godless greed with T&A. I could muster fondness for programming that admitted such a thing. The show has been presided over in its most popular years by Bob Barker, silver-haired animal activist who forces his obsession ("Have your pet spayed or neutered") on viewers whenever he's not off-camera defending himself against accusations of allegedly coming on to more than one of the "Barker's Beauties" hostesses, who are, ultimately, the only reason to watch this loud, vulgar display.

Love

Infomercials: All the Stuff You Don't Need . . . Buy It Now and We'll Throw In This Set of Steak Knives!

Praise be to the infomercial, TV capitalism at its most direct, unironic, and entertaining. Who among us has not spent hours amused and enlightened by Ron Popeil, who is the Cary Grant, the Fred Astaire, of the infomercial, with his utterly debonair demonstration of his "Showtime Rotisserie" Who has not watched goggle-eyed as the far-more-goggle-eyed-than-me-and-thee Matthew Lesko yammers on and on about how he can save you thousands of dollars with "free stuff" you can locate, but if only you buy his not-free book revealing the secrets (a perfect commodity tautology). I have even permitted myself to be lulled by the creamy voice of former *Dynasty* star Linda Evans extol the virtues of "Rejuvenique," almost forgetting that what she's pitching is a plastic mask hooked up to a nine-volt battery as a marvelous way to exercise and smooth out your/my face.

Let's, um, face it: infomercials are the not-at-all-guilty pleasure of the upper-middlebrow consumer. That is to say, many of us who would not be caught dead roaming the self-help section of a bookstore happily turn over thirty minutes or an hour of our time to the promises of better health, more easily cooked food, and creamier skin as presented by the best infomercial pitch-people. And there are standards even here. Popeil, a truly amazing only-in-America entrepreneur, has invented everything from the Pocket Fisherman to the Inside-the-Shell Egg Scrambler, tests the products himself, and then goes on the air to personally instruct and sell his creations. While Popeil is at the summit of Infomercial Mountain, the sherpas schlepping up that mountain yelling about how tough it is are the yeoman screamers like Lesko and the exceedingly off-putting Tony Little, the ponytailed muscleman who shouts incessantly about crap exercise equipment like the gliding-your-way-to-the-chiropractor ab-building item the Gazelle Freestyle. Oh, and Miss Cleo—sorry, baby, don't believe the Tarot cards any more than I do your accent.

If the most famous infomercial is probably Suzanne Somers and her Thigh-Master, that's only because we like to see how far once-prominent celebrities have fallen. (Most scary: Somers's *Three's Company* replacement Jenilee Harrison, shrunken and gaunt from, I can only presume, one of the numerous products she's advocating, such as the "total body fitness machine," the Power Gym, which looks as if it could snap Harrison's brittle bones with one crunch.)

I have no use for an all-infomercial channel like QVC, with its assembly-line approach to hawking things like zircon jewelry and "Keepsake" scrapbooks. Its hosts are slickly insincere, and most of them try so hard to relate to phone-in callers, to feign affection, concern, and empathy for the consumers' desires, that these on-air shills quickly become hateful little toadies. I also avoid the business gurus epitomized by Tony Robbins, the Gigantor of get-rich-quick confidence-building. Robbins exudes a ferocious intensity comparable only to Scientology recruiters who've landed time with a mark who's just purchased his first L. Ron Hubbard title. No, I like my infomercials the old-fashioned way: in the dead of night, when the line between need and desire had been blurred by insomnia, isolation, and a depressant-or-stimulant-of-choice. It's then that the honey-eyed tones of the admirable Mr. Popeil, or the enduring *Dallas* charm of Victoria Principal, is most persuasive. Mind you, I've never actually been drunk enough to pull out my credit card and dial the 800 number, but the fact that I can be nudged along to even contemplate it is a measure of how good this sort of TV can be. And in the pre-dawn hours, it beats the hell out of one of NBC's post-post-late-night *Tonight Show* reruns, or an actual *Three's Company* on Nick At Nite.

Hate

The Slow, Steady Decline of *The Tonight Show* Even as It Becomes More Popular

What's that? You say you don't care about *The Tonight Show*? Just proves my point: Under the current stewardship of Jay Leno, the late-night institution has become a shrill shill-fest, with the host glad-handing audience members at the opening of every edition in one of the least spontaneous interactions between star and spectators ever devised. Leno was once a first-rate stand-up comic who used to slay nightclub crowds as well as studio tourists when he did his patented "What's my beef?" routines with his former buddy on *Late Night with David Letterman*. He has since willed himself to become a chucklehead. This, even as he does potentially sharp regular routines like "Jaywalking," in which Leno goes out on the street and by asking the simplest questions proves that ordinary folk are so poorly educated, they don't know government officials' names or any fragment of history older than the last edition of *Survivor*. Such first-hand contact—you'll never catch the shy, compulsively aloof

Letterman mingling with the hoi polloi outside of a studio—must only increase a contempt for his viewers that is communicated via Leno's increasingly vulgar humor: Bill Clinton is invariably a fat cheating slob; Nick Nolte will die with Leno still making disgraceful, too-easy fun of the actor's sad police mug shot. And there is Leno's unstated admission that no guest is on his couch other than to plug his/her latest product and serve the precooked anecdote elicited by Leno's backstage warm-up handlers.

Leno's detractors often compare him to his predecessor, Johnny Carson (host from 1962 to 1992), and, to be semifair, nearly all late-night hosts pay unctuous obeisance to King Carson. Sorry, boys: Johnny, while obviously superior to Leno in being better at feigning interest and laughter at guests' babble—may have been more smoothly skilled than Jay, but he's also dreadfully overrated. Most of Carson's greatest hits—his 1965 glee when guest Ed Ames accidentally threw a tomahawk that landed near the crotch of an outlined-figure target (Johnny's ad lib: "I didn't even know you were Jewish": groan); his scampering leap into announcer Ed McMahon's arms when a guest cougar growled at him—can now be seen as obviously staged bits. Carson stole his "Aunt Blabby" character from Jonathan Winters's Maude Fricker; the "Stump the Band" routine from his predecessor, Steve Allen.

The fact that Carson stayed at it for so long—thirty-one years—has much to do with Carson's inflated rep (Jack Paar, who held the post for a mere five, once told Carson with typically razor-edged rue, "I wish I'd only rented you the job—or married you"). From late-blooming boomers on, millions now cannot remember the pre-Carson *Tonight Show*, and so don't recall that the late-'70s-to-late-'80s was a fallow period for Carson. He was increasingly out of touch, with his wide-lapelled suits drawn from the closet of his own clothing line (do you know *anyone* who ever bought one of those heavily *Tonight Show*–advertised Carson suits?), mildly contemptuous of post-Beatles popular culture (for mild contempt was all Carson ever allowed himself to display on-camera, though his multiple, non-Paar marriages suggest a deeper well of resentment); his monologues slowed to a series of "It was so hot today . . . ," followed by the audience's chant, "How hot was it?" He doled out yuks and the sort of bipartisan political humor whose toothlessness was exceeded only by the gummy suck-up of a Bob Hope TV routine.

The outpouring of hosannas when Carson announced his retirement was certainly a canny late-period career move, resulting in a surge in ratings and respect. Suddenly younger writers on the TV beat started showering Carson with the sort of praise accorded to someone they thought must be a giant, primarily because they'd never seen one. Letterman had come along, appearing at first as a wiseass who injected just enough irony and self-parody into the talk-show format that he looked like a young turk. (The cruel aging process never stops, of course: These days, Conan O'Brien and Jon Stewart can sometimes make Letterman look mummified in mannerism, stuck doing Top 10 lists until his eyes give out. Of course, I believe this is the ever-canny Letterman's strategy: he has willingly, wisely surrendered ironic-rebel status for a middle-aged-crazy style that suits his complex, brooding persona.)

By the time Carson broadcast his final two shows in May of 1992, it seemed to many as though the clever-young-man-turned-silver-haired-automaton was a miracle we'd never witness again. When Johnny teared up as Bette Midler serenaded him on the penultimate show, it was tantamount to seeing the Mount Rushmore

Abe Lincoln emit moisture from his cold, stone eyes. Carson's most brilliant performance occurred after *The Tonight Show,* when he disappeared from public view, his absence only enhancing the myth that he was the greatest host ever. By declining to seek reassurance of audience-love, he attained mystical allure. Rumors of a regular poker game resounded like reports of gods gathering at Valhalla—no matter that those seated at his green felt table included Steve Martin, Carl Reiner, and . . . Chevy Chase. Chevy Chase? Host of the most welcome talk-show debacle in history—one month on Fox in 1993? The man of whom even King Carson had said, "Chevy couldn't ad-lib a fart after a baked bean dinner"? How did the most despised member of *Saturday Night Live*, the *National Lampoon's Vacation* boob, kiss Carson's ass so tenderly as to be admitted to the sacred circle? And, oh, yes: Carson's one bit of entertainment in his retirement years has been to write the occasional humor "casual" for *The New Yorker*. They are notably unfunny.

We must continue to work backward, in order to keep progressing to greatness. Jack Paar (1957–1962) was a brilliantly mercurial character, an egotist tempered by his prodigious sentimental streak. Only Letterman is Paar's equal as a complex, moody personality—traits that would, in a lesser performer, have worked against him as a gracious host. Yet Paar stands as a remarkable creation of television, chatty rather than witty, eager to let the guest do the heavy lifting of entertaining, visually a curious-looking specimen, with an enormously high forehead and long, splay-tipped, ET-like fingers. No one ever mentions this, but there was also something fascinatingly effeminate about the way Paar carried himself, gestured, and, of course, cried at the drop of a sad piano note, or a melancholy anecdote from any member of the Kennedy political family he adored.

Paar was too fragile a talent to withstand the rigors of smiling at third-rate celebs most nights, or plumbing his personal life for opening-moment anecdotes rather than the current-events snickers his successors went for. One of Paar's joke-writers was a fledgling Dick Cavett, another hothouse flower who, in a different way, on a different network (self-impressed and ABC, respectively) would flame onto the scene and flame out. Paar himself would try a couple of less adventurous and popular shows, retire for good, emerge occasionally to be interviewed by his lesser colleagues, and give encouragement to, among others, Conan O'Brien at that early time when few other pros, let alone members of the same profession, could imagine the ginger-haired youth surviving, let alone flourishing. Paar was canny to the end, which was 2004.

But back, back, finally: To Steve Allen, whose 1954–1957 *Tonight Show* is the closest to perfection, or at least the complete synthesis-DNA of what would follow: opening jokes, followed by skits or stunts, followed by a couple of guests, interrupted by surprises. Allen possessed the mien of a hip Ivy League prof, using his black hornrims (then signifiers of seriousness and education) to become a one-man straight-man and clown. He'd yank off his specs to deliver a multisyllabic or non sequitur mock-tirade. One of his best semiregular *Tonight Show* routines was reading newspaper copy; not the funny-headlines crap that Leno uses to get brute laughter from crude typos. Allen simply took irate letters written to the editor and read them in the indignant tone Allen imagined the author to have had in his or her head when the letter was penned.

Unlike Paar and Carson, when Allen left the *Tonight Show* he stayed around too long, slowly becoming the sort of stuffy windbag he used to parody. True, post-*Tonight*, his Sunday night *Steve Allen*

Show was a magnificent but ultimately doomed effort to outdraw Ed Sullivan in the ratings. This one, not *Tonight*, is where Allen assembled his great rep company of comedians like Louie Nye, Don Knotts, and Tom Poston. A decent piano player, Allen used the instrument for crisp comic punctuation and to showcase the jazz artists he loved. He eventually came to take unwarranted pride in having written thousands of songs, of which "This Could Be the Start of Something Big" is the only one that became well known, and scores of mediocre fiction and nonfiction books. Add the fact that NBC destroyed the majority of his *Tonight Show* kinescopes by foolish accident or neglect, and it's difficult to prove to the young that Allen was once the hippest cat to host a mass-broadcast talk show, the guy who took cameras out on the street to pull crazy stunts before Letterman, who could ad-lib with audience members more hilariously than any host since.

Leno strives mightily to make it look as though he's—well, striving mightily. He glitzed up the *Tonight Show* stage so that his entrances are like modern carnival come-ons, treating the studio audience as though they were suckers to be jovially fleeced. He works out new material in night clubs, touring the country glad-handing affiliates and doing corporate gigs even though he's past his early prime of expressing enjoyment in his labor and isn't doing it for the dough. Allen made it look easy, as though he was making it up as he went along. Which he sort-of was.

Love

Roseanne: Undomesticated Goddess

Roseanne Barr/Arnold/So-famous-needs-no-surname ranks with Jackie Gleason and Lucille Ball as one of television's few utterly self-created innovators. Like Gleason's *Honeymooners*, her *Roseanne* (1988–1997) was, right up through its final very odd, surreal season, a working-class comedy the humor of which derived from the dank despair of its struggling laborers. Like Ball, Roseanne was a behind-the-scenes innovator and controller, who oversaw much of the writing and producing. Both knew that women who exerted strong opinions had to be very tough and very creative. Like Gleason, she surrounded herself with costars—in particular John Goodman as her gruff, loving, argumentative, striving-yet-unlucky-in-life husband and Laurie Metcalf as her gruff, loving, less argumentative than resigned striving-yet-unlucky-in-life-and-love sister—who got as many laughs as the star did, and the star knew This Was Good.

Beyond this, however, Roseanne is unique: imperious yet quick to wound, intellectually insecure and autodidactically learned, ruthlessly sensible and gleefully, self-aware-wacky. Her show, *Roseanne,* could have been like one of the scores of sitcoms built around the persona of its stand-up-comic star. In Roseanne's case, she referred to herself in nightclubs and talk-shows as a "domestic goddess," a phrase freighted with malicious irony, since off-stage and on-screen, Roseanne assiduously ignored or despised the petty work required of the vast majority of wives and mothers. The series' out-of-the-box success was due to that wonder of pop-culture: a public that didn't realize *this* was what it wanted to see and hear at this moment until it came into their living rooms.

Roseanne Connor's family, with its dowdier-than-*All in the Family* furniture, its incessant squabbling, followed by hugs and subtle affirmations of each other's self-worth, a household in which brutal honesty was required, exhausting and exhilarating simultaneously, was remarkably nuanced. No other sitcom made the effort to pay the bills so engrossing.

We bring to the experience of watching not merely our knowledge of the characters but also everything we know about the stars' private lives. In this area, Roseanne was even more of a phenomenon than her contemporary, Madonna. It was impossible *not* to know when Roseanne divorced her pre-stardom husband, Bill Pentland, took up with a third-rate comic, Tom Arnold, sang a scandalously out-of-tune version of the national anthem at a baseball game, proclaimed a multiple-personality disorder, accused her father of child abuse, or took to studying the Kabbalah. There were reports of constant behind-the-scenes creative turmoil resulting in her incessant firing of writers and producers. "I used to surround myself with people I could pick fights with, 'cause it was all about winning; I was so screwed up," she once told me. She turned the show on its head in the final months so that Roseanne Connor became immensely wealthy and acted out any number of nouveau-riche fantasies that were progressively less amusing to the public than they seemed to be to the star herself until *Roseanne* pretty much disappeared up its own rear end. All this coheres not as the career of a TV star but as something deeper and richer—the journey of Roseanne. She'd be the first to sneer at this use of the sentimentalizing, hackneyed use of the word "journey," and you can tune in to syndicated reruns of the early seasons of *Roseanne* for a ferocious counterpoint. These episodes remain fresh in their slap-in-the-face honesty about the strains of marriage when two people work hard all day, about how difficult it is to pay attention to the emotional growth spurts and withdrawals of your children when you're preoccupied thinking about how to grab some overtime money, about how love and fury constantly commingle under the roof of a too-small, messy house. This is the triumph of *Roseanne*, and Roseanne.

Hate

The Smothers Brothers: The Revolutionaries Who Bombed

Tom and Dick Smothers are the variety-show version of the Weather Underground: unfocused revolutionaries, smug, self-immolating and self-pitying (particularly in the case of Tom) and not without delusions of grandeur. When the brothers began their CBS variety show in 1967, they were familiar TV faces, adept at harmless folk-song parodies and assiduously zany banter. Tom played the wise-cracking dummy to Dick's calm, intelligent-seeming straight-man, and Tom's "Mom always liked you best!" routine was the duo's trademark knee-slapper. *The Comedy Hour* was not without talent— its writing staff included Steve Martin, Mason Williams, who wrote good comedy if not good music, as his dreadful 1968 instrumental hit "Classical Gas" attests; Bob Einstein, brother of Albert Brooks and the future "Super Dave Osborne"; and Rob Reiner. On-camera, deadpan comic Pat Paulsen was amusing well before he ran his "Pat

Paulsen for President" routine into the ground, David Steinberg was a regular guest when he was still a sharp-witted, enjoyably smart-alecky young stand-up, a Dennis Miller with content and without the ranting.

Right from the start the brothers, particularly Tom, tried to bring a countercultural sensibility to prime time, which was not ready for it—indeed, network television would never be ready for the sort of revolution in form and content that was routinely occurring in rock music at the time. *The Comedy Hour* premiered, it's instructive to realize, the same year that the Beatles' *Sgt. Pepper's Lonely Hearts Club Band* was released. On the Smothers' first show, CBS refused to let a guest the brothers had requested, folk singer Pete Seeger, sing "Waist Deep in the Big Muddy" because of its obvious anti–Vietnam War message.

On one hand, the Smothers Brothers knew they were dealing with an inherently conservative medium—that's why for every Buffalo Springfield or Jefferson Airplane who appeared, there was a George Gobel or an Anthony Newley. Old-guard show-biz "balanced," in the eyes and ears of the Tiffany Network, the scruffy dissenters the Smothers were using their solid ratings—the best CBS had seen on their Sunday-night, up-against-*Bonanza* time period in years—to force onto the airwaves. For the record, the Airplane was always a lousy band in performance, even when lip-synching, and Gobel's well-told shaggy-dog stories hold up as better popular art.

Soon, the never-very-private squabbling between network and stars—who were capable of very silly forms of rebellion, for example the insipid "pot" jokes of the "Have a Little Tea with Goldie" segments—took its toll on both ends. CBS became more ridiculously censorious, as the Smothers' work grew increasingly, doomingly, heavy-handed. Petulant and self-righteous, Tommy gave tedious interviews castigating the network, and the brothers even went on a rival network, NBC and its *Tonight Show*, to air some sketches that CBS had nixed. Oooh, how *daring*: using Johnny Carson's show as a platform for revolution! The initial minor thrill of seeing the Smothers Brothers flash the V-fingered peace sign and Pat Paulsen's intentionally mangled diatribes about freedom of speech eventually turned-off viewers in every sense, and the brothers left the air in '69. Dick started making his own wine—one imagines that's how badly he felt he needed to get a drink, and some distance from his hectoring sibling. Tommy has been milking the Smothers-as-vanguard-artists legend ever since, but anyone who actually looks at those shows now will see a lot of stuff that's grimly, perversely proudly, unfunny.

Love

David Brinkley as the Only TV News Anchor Who Realized That News Anchoring Is a Crock

David Brinkley (1920–2003)—co-anchor with Chet Huntley of *The Huntley-Brinkley Report* (1956–1971); wizened-apple-head host of *This Week With David Brinkley* (1981–1996)—communicated most effectively the sage understanding that being a news anchor was a position of false authority, suppressed thought and emotion, and constant capitulation between the news, the network, the public, and the sponsor. He was a man of principle: When the American Federation of Television and Radio Artists (AFTRA) called for a strike in 1967, Brinkley and Huntley, both union members were asked by NBC to cross the picket line. Huntley obeyed his masters while Brinkley told them, in effect, to bug off. As Jeff Alan reports in his book *Anchoring America* (2003), the front page of the New York *Daily News* read CHET TALKS, DAVE WALKS.

Brinkley was distinctive among news anchors. He wrote his own copy and did it well, crafting stories as though they were crisp New York Times dispatches, and then delivered them with that idiosyncratic sonorousness, with its stop-start emphatic verbal punctuation. Walter Cronkite—an admirable man himself, for his outspokenness and independence of thought—became at once excessively revered and condescendingly marginalized as "Uncle Walter," America's "most trusted" man. Brinkley bypassed this sort of adulation, and was all the better for it. The best, in fact.

Hate

The Cult of Edward R. Murrow

There is probably no figure more universally revered in television history than newsman Edward R. Murrow. Emerging from radio in the '40s, Murrow along with such producers as Fred Friendly and future *60 Minutes* boss Don Hewett perfected a certain sort of documentary newscast. While claiming to hew to the most rigorous, "objective" standards of journalism, Ed and the so-called "Murrow's Boys," a team of correspondents that included Eric Sevareid, Howard K. Smith, and Charles Collingwood, made their newscasts personal in tone and point of view. Murrow, valorized now as a self-sacrificing crusader, is actually, when you look at the tapes, a prototypical TV star. He stares out at the audience with his jaw kept tucked in, like a prizefighter, looking up and into the camera, enunciating his words with exaggerated emphasis. Early on, he became famous not so much for what he was reporting on the London blitz in 1940, but for the way he introduced his reports: "*This* . . . [pause for dramatic effect] is Trafalgar Square," he'd say. With his impeccably tailored suits and an ever-present cigarette used to extend pauses or make a punctuational point when flicked aside, Murrow was as much of a performer as any entertainment figure.

It's difficult to believe now—as we pass the era of dashin' Dan Rather throwing his wacky Texas truisms into election-night analysis, or find ourselves watching a news magazine like *60 Minutes* or *Dateline* that are as likely to profile the director of a summer blockbuster as they are to traffick in actual news—that to suggest that Murrow was a showboater as well as a reporter would have brought hisses a half-century ago. If Murrow had his "boys," he was The Man: The jacket-and-tie version of *Gunsmoke*'s Marshall Dillon, he had faced down Sen. Joe McCarthy and supposedly exposed the sweaty Red-baiter for the craven jackel he was. What Murrow really did was make his point about McCarthy's unworthiness not via closely reasoned argument, but by exposing McCarthy as a singularly untelegenic human, editing the big toad to look haltingly unsure, and capping it with a pious speech that now sounds startlingly wishy-washy, including the sentence, "This is no time for men who oppose Senator McCarthy's methods to keep silent—or for those who approve." In other words: "Hey, everybody's got his opinion— you may like this sullen bully who's destroying people's lives." This is a high point of crusading journalism on TV? Sounds like a man revealing himself for what he was: a privileged insider who was good buddies with the boss, CBS founder Bill Paley.

Really, much of what Murrow was doing was developing the tele-visual tropes that make so much TV news now unbearable. His reports from Germany in the aftermath of World War II were hailed as newscasts that tried to place the horror of war in perspective. Of course, any time TV tries to do that, it avoids the true obscenity of war's violence. Gotta abide by the network's standards-and-practices, as well as the sponsors' middlebrow notions of good taste, lest some little old man in the Midwest get upset. It's also little-remembered now that when Murrow got around to McCarthy, the newsman had been criticized by many inside and outside the news industry as arriving as the Chain-Smoking Avenger a little late. McCarthy had already wrecked a lot of lives by the time Murrow and Friendly got around to him in 1954.

When we sneer at a Barbara Walters for mixing interviews with heads of state with fawning interrogations of Oscar nominees, well, Murrow was a sell-out, too, hosting a celebrity suck-up series, *Person to Person*, doing his best Humphrey Bogart–worldweariness joshing with Marilyn Monroe, and acting as though he had to slum like that to keep doing his harder-news *See It Now*. Eric Barnouw notes in his history *Tube of Plenty: The Evolution of American Television* (1975) that one of his *Person to Person* guests, actor-director John Cassavetes, himself always torn between art, commerce, and a good cigarette—Murrow as Method Actor—asked Murrow why he did the celeb stuff. The reply? "To do the show I want to do, I have to do the show I don't want to do." Well, that's probably a more succinct version of what Stone Phillips tells himself at night, too. Except he probably thinks, "To get a classy Spielberg interview, I have to do a David Gest to grab some easy ratings."

From his puffed-up first-person narration to his movie-star cool, Murrow was a reporter who seems to have liked the attention as much as the journalism. If he was around today, he'd probably sub for Baba Wawa on *The View*, Meredith Viera would think he was super-cute, and Murrow probably wouldn't do anything to dissuade her. It would beat hanging out with the "boys."

Love

**Best Use of an Insane Evangelical: Alec Baldwin in *Knots Landing*
(1984–1985)**

First of all, all proper respect to *Knots Landing*, the nut-nut-nuttiest
'80s-era nighttime soap from the production factory that defined the
genre, Spelling-Goldberg. This spin-off from *Dallas*, for my money,
is better than the source-show. If only for Joan van Ark's jaw-
droppingly gullible Valene Ewing and TV's most realistically neurotic novelist (remember, Val was the author of the successful
potboiler *Capricorn Crude*), if only for Donna Mills's gigantic-haired
vixen Abby, if only for William Devane's gleaming-choppers shark-
grin as real-estate developer Greg Summer, if only for Ted Shack-
elford's most dependable on-and-off-the-wagon alkie, if only for the
black-sheep Ewing, Gary—for these and so many more marvelously
shlock pleasures, *Knots Landing* stands as TV's finest purveyor of
suburban cul-de-sac huggermugger.

The fourteen-year run of the show peaked about midway
through, when a dewy-eyed tiger-cub of an actor—the prebulked-
out Alec Baldwin—scampered through a primo story arc as Joshua
Rich, a nutso evangelist. He only had baby-blues for Lisa Hartman's
Cathy, a would-be pop star brought in through the back door of a
subplot involving Val's press agent, who represented them both.

Hartman, who would go on to become country crooner Clint
Black's wife and was at the time trying to sustain a real-life music career (four mawkishly middle-of-the-road pop-rock albums between

'76 and '87), was good at wide-eyed innocence. It's no wonder she fell for the messianic spiel of Baldwin's rush. One of our first glimpses of him is Joshua preaching to a mesmerized crowd in an L.A. supermarket parking lot. "Oh my God!" says a horrified Michele Lee, the series' sole sane character and impeccable presenter of the show's middle-class mores: preaching in a parking lot—how horribly tacky!

Baldwin played Joshua and his evangelism as though he were assaying Howard Roarke in *The Fountainhead*—that is, far above the true level of the material, fully aware that his character is a pathetic-on-the-inside, boldly-greedy-on-the-outside character. At the time, televangelists like Jim Bakker and Pat Robertson were still going strong. He brings Hartman's Cathy into his flock, singling her out for her bod but wooing her for her spirit, conducting a season-long rant about how he and the would-be star must become "one." He begins overseeing her demo session, much as Brian Wilson's career was hijacked by another dubious spiritual advisor/therapist, Dr. Eugene Landy. Joshua repeatedly said that he and Cathy were meant for each other. She thought he meant marriage. We knew he meant leaping to their death from a building-top together as a way to cement literally a legendary status and attain the Higher Plane. Spiralling out of control, Joshua and his madness become evident even to the blindingly ambitious Cathy, who tries to break it off. When he brings her to the rooftop, she cunningly but graciously allows him to fall first, and Baldwin left the series with a splat.

Soon after, Hartman abandoned her faux–Pat Benatar look and meekly returned to the *Knots* neighborhood. Baldwin took all that carefully modulated pent-up rage and used it to fuel a great, unheralded movie performance, as the amoral thug Junior in the brilliant 1990 B movie *Miami Blues*. By that same year, *Knots* was in its death throes, lurching from one unamusingly absurd plot to another, but Baldwin's spiralling fall had lifted *Knots Landing*, if only for a moment, to nighttime-soap nirvana.

Hate

Vincent D'Onofrio: Or, What if Marlon Brando and Columbo Had Had a Baby?

The *Law & Order* franchise is characterized by self-contained, hourlong tales enacted by casts who prize either pithy tartness (think Sam Waterston in the crispy, clear-eyed original) or succinct bluntness (think Ice-T in the soggier, weepier *Special Victims Unit*). The actors are very much ensemble players—indeed, producer Dick Wolf demands that this be so, if only because, for reasons of verisimilitude and, more important, economics, Wolf needs his squad rooms and courtrooms to be populated with equal-opportunity players who can be moved or replaced in the space of a season.

But in *Law & Order: Criminal Intent*, which premiered in 2001, Wolf broke with his own tradition. *Criminal Intent* shows you the crime first, then lets you watch how the heroes suss it all out. The series is centered around one police investigator, Det. Goren, played by Vincent D'Onofrio—a "special case squad" mystery-solver. D'Onofrio reveals the workings of his character's mind by physicalizing everything. He doesn't just interrogate someone, he bends his long, wide, Gumby body around a suspect, who becomes unnerved when D'Onofrio waggles a frankfurter-long finger in his face and asks cutting yet smiley-faced questions. Back at the station house, his primary audience is his woefully underused costar, Kathryn Erbe, as he does a lot of mock-anguished face-pulling while trying to figure out a suspect's motives. Goren, like Columbo, wears rumpled suits and behaves in a distracted manner, leading some to think he's just an eccentric bumbler, but he's always thinking the case through. He comes back with a just-one-more-question-please inquiry that inevitably startles suspects.

There have been other *L&O* regulars who've worked extensively in the theater and in movies—Waterston, Jerry Orbach, Courtney B. Vance—but none of them comes at it with the neo-Method approach of D'Onofrio, who broke into movies in a big way as a refrigerator-sized recruit in Stanley Kubrick's 1987 *Full Metal Jacket*. Part Brando with his off-the-wall mannerism, the voice pitched too high for his body mass; part Peter Falk with his pretended folksiness and sudden swerves into gimlet-eyed shrewdness, D'Onofrio is, in a word, insufferable.

Sure, the first few times you watch him, he's fun, but very quickly you realize what the actor is doing is just plain camera-hogging, and the writers only encourage him. Erbe must have 75 percent less dialogue than D'Onofrio. Her primary function is to stand around and watch him, feigning fascination, which, pro that she is, she does very well as D'Onofrio does an all-stops-out ham-bone performance. It's distracting, it's derivative, it's not a de-lovely sight to see. It goes against the grain of what *Law & Order* is all about—people laboring together to avenge the rights of others.

Criminal Intent also becomes a metaphor for early-twenty-first-century selfishness: *My* intentions, says D'Onofrio's performance, are more worthy than yours, than that of my costars' or even my own character's. What matters, in this actor's interpretation, is me, me, me. I, he says implicitly, will elevate a standard TV show. After all, this medium is lucky to have me at all—why, I've done Kubrick, *Men In Black*, and indie films! I will bestow my largesse upon the couch potatoes by showing everyone up and showing off. Unlike Alec Baldwin, who paid his dues in TV and worked gradually toward being a show-offy star few people wanted to hire, D'Onofrio began as a praised film actor who's become a show-offy star his employers are afraid to discipline.

Love

The Joy of Painting: **Bob Ross as the Mister Rogers of Impressionism**

"Let's just put some happy little trees over here, shall we?" And indeed we shall. With his speckled hand holding a two-inch-wide brush, painter Bob Ross daubs on a canvas a mixture of brown and orange with quick strokes—I'd say "stabbing motions" if the verb didn't go against everything his 403-episode instructional-painting show stood for, so let's use "firm darting motions." Ross, the son of a Florida carpenter, and who died in 1995, did as much to sooth jangling TV viewers' nerves as Mr. Rogers by teaching simple but genuine, fundamental painting techniques to millions.

Sure, his subject matter is limited to land- and seascapes with titles like "Pretty Autumn Day," and no one's going to make the case for Ross as anything more than a canny teacher cum entrepreneur. His line of painting supplies remains a multimillion-dollar business. Even so, the guy provided a lot of pleasure, knowledge, and encouragement to people who might otherwise never enter an art gallery or pick up a brush.

For most of *The Joy of Painting*'s existence on public-television stations across the country, Ross was a trim white man with a bushy brown Afro and a white-speckled beard. He'd superimpose on the screen the colors you'd need to do each painting at the start of the show—"titanium white"; "yellow ochre"—commence with a blank canvas prepared "wet," that is, presoaked in white or black paint, the easier to absorb and fast-dry the colors he applied. He showed you how to hold a brush and cradle a palette containing tube-squirts of paint, how to use a flat-edged knife to mix and separate the colors, and, most of all, how to get started. What could be more elemental to the creative process than grappling with that phrase that has become the cliché of every sort of artist, from painter to novelist to filmmaker—"the blank canvas."

Ross just dove right in, telling viewers, "You are the master of this canvas," adding, "Of course, I am a firm believer that you can do anything in life." Watching a man start and finish a complete painting in just under thirty minutes in every edition of *The Joy of Painting*, you rarely thought, "Boy, he sure churns the junk out, doesn't he?" More likely, you thought, "Hey, I could do that, too!" Yet that notion wasn't expressed as the sort of contemptuous, my-kid-can-paint-better-than-Jackson-Pollock attitude of your average Neanderthal with an SUV; Ross's anyone-can-do-it painting instruction wasn't exclusionary or polemical. Off-camera he was dismissive of abstract modern art, telling *The New York Times* in 1991, "If I paint something, I don't want to have to explain what it is."

Ross, working out of the Muncie, Indiana, public TV station where he taped his shows, spoke in a low-register murmur as he painted with quick authority, popping a mountain against a skyline and exclaiming, with traces of his Southern Florida accent still intact, "Oooh, I like '*at!*" Ross preached community without being preachy—since he had to keep talking as he filled in his umpteenth "happy little cloud." When adding a green bush next to a brown one, he'd say things like, "Everybody should have a friend, at least one, preferably two or three." This affable nattering was a big part of Ross's success—that, and the fact that he was doing something useful. So much about art-making is a mystery to the layman. How do you stretch a canvas? What's the difference between oils and acrylics? What size paintbrush would I use in a given situation? That knowledge is usually, infuriatingly, held back as too obvious to reveal to us by professionals. Only Andy Warhol was as unpretentious about the manufacturing of art as Ross was. But try getting Josef Albers to explain how to paint a landscape and all he'd deliver was a black mountain of theory.

Don't misunderstand. My artistic hero is the German Dada-era "Merz"-master Kurt Schwitters, and I'd rather read the art criticism of Dave Hickey and Sanford Schwartz than the latest John Grisham. In other words, I'm not Ross's ideal audience. What I connect to is Ross's sense of the *democracy of art*—the sense that, like rock music and a lot of TV, art should be something anyone can make without feeling intimidated. Sure, most of Ross's landscapes are barely worthy of being hung in a garage, but I learned a lot about the basics of painterly technique that far greater artists or even teachers find it beneath them to articulate.

And here's the clean little secret of Bob Ross's landscapes: While you can clearly recognize what he said his son Steve called his "mooshes" of paint-on-canvas as a tree or a pebbly beach, they aren't realistic representations—Ross was teaching a variation on Impressionism. He used general shapes and perspectives that led our eyes and minds to take in his daubed blobs as items in nature. Yep, Bob Ross was an abstractionist at bottom, and I like him for 'at.

And so I conclude as Ross did, directing his own parting message back at him: "Happy painting and God bless, my friend."

Hate

Saturday Night Live: The Myth of
Michael O'Donoghue's Genius

What can you say about a comedy writer whose claim to fame is a running gag in which he puts long sewing needles into his eyes and his most subtle bon mot is a put-down of the Muppets ("I won't write for felt")? Well, you can paraphrase Franklin P. Adams and say that satire is what dies on *Saturday Night*. O'Donoghue, dark prince of *National Lampoon* when it was a cutting-edge magazine, brought his black humor to the first seasons of *SNL*. Like a lot of brooding entertainment types who act as though they're biting the hand that feeds them while gorging on the meal, he got away with a lot of sophomoric stuff. O'Donoghue, who died in 1994, specialized in the vaguely sinister non sequitur. The debut edition of *SNL* consisted of O'Donoghue and John Belushi enacting a surreal scenario built around lines like, "I would like to feed your fingertips to the wolverines." I think Andre Breton got to that place about a half-century earlier than O'Donoghue did.

In Tom Shales and James Andrew Miller's invaluable oral history of *Saturday Night Live, Live From New York* (2002), O'Donoghue's ex-girlfriend, writer Anne Beatts, refers to him as "Cardinal Richelieu . . . the person plotting revolution or the power behind the king"—that would be Lorne Michaels. But O'Donoghue's idea of being subversive was to suggest putting musical guest ABBA on a *Titanic* set and make it look as though the Swedish popsters were drowning: Oooh, daaarrring! For a writer, O'Donoghue also sucked on the printed page. His short-lived column for *Spin* magazine took easy potshots at Liza Minnelli and slurs against "the Arabs—any race that eats with one hand and wipes with the other is bound to become confused occasionally." He dug homophobe jokes, too. Gee, whatta revolutionary. The more you look closely at that first generation of *SNL*ers (and I'm putting Bill Murray in the second generation), they were, with the exception of Dan Aykroyd, highly overrated guys. And I do mean guys—O'Donoghue couldn't, or wouldn't, write anything of quality for female cast members. Thus began *SNL*'s two worst legacies. Those would be, in John Belushi's case, drug abuse, and in O'Donoghue's, the myth of the writer as taboo breaker. What he really was was a smug potty mouth. Tina Fey has written more "subversive" humor for *SNL* than O'Donoghue ever did, may he rest in the troubled peace he so desired.

Love

The Jack Benny Program

Everybody over age forty remembers a few things about Jack Benny: He played the violin, he always gave his age as thirty-nine, and his comic persona was that of a cheapskate. His most quoted TV joke was his answer to a robber who demanded "Your money or your life!" After a long pause and the robber's repeated threat, Benny responds, "I'm thinking it over!" When nonplussed, the comedian held his hand to his cheek and exclaimed, "*Well!*" with the sort of plush emphasis that might remind people today of either Kelsey Grammer, who has paid generous homage to Benny's influence in a 1995 best-of special, or *Queer Eye for the Straight Guy*'s Carson Kressley.

Anyone *under* the age of forty can also appreciate Jack Benny's beautifully calm yet neurotic comic image, along with the TV show he created around it, as more nuanced and innovative than his greatest hits or nostalgia would have you think. I was struck, when Bob Hope died in 2003, by one repeatedly-aired clip from a TV special that was supposed to display Hope's skill as an ad-libber who cracked up his colleagues. But it was Benny who gets the biggest laugh by looking straight at the camera, breaking free from the script and declaring flatly, "This is the *stupid*est thing I've ever been in!" It was that sort of directness—not rudeness, not insult comedy, just well-timed exasperation, the communication of how foolish an enterprise one may be involved in at any given moment—that makes *The Jack Benny Program* (1950–1964) durable. You can watch old episodes (though try and find 'em—it's either The Museums of Television in Manhattan and Los Angeles, or the Internet) and re-enter a disappeared world of nuttiness and decorum, of standards established and not met, to the rue of the man in charge.

To be sure, Benny had a raft of writers behind him, but it was his sensibility that guided the crafting of the jokes. In one of his shows, he and guest star Vincent Price drank some freshly brewed coffee. After savoring a sip, Benny announced, "This is the better coffee I ever tasted." Price snapped, "You mean the *best* coffee!" Benny snapped back, "There's only *two* of us drinking it!" Who makes grammar jokes anymore, let alone ones that still echo with the punchline's original ringing laughter?

Comedian Fred Allen, with whom Benny conducted a mock-feud for years, observed that Benny was one of the first radio and TV comics who got his laughs by letting people make fun of him, as opposed to his making fun of a gaggle of supporting-cast stooges. This is especially true of his greatest comic partner, Eddie "Rochester" Anderson. Rochester—valet and chauffeur—was a parody of the menial character black actors had endured over decades of show biz. Benny's show broke the stereotype by having Rochester not only be quicker and smarter about the real world than Jack, but also gave him a rounded personality. In his off-hours, it was made clear, Rochester led a life, with relationships his employer knew nothing about, and an attitude toward that employer that wasn't nearly as generous and sunny as Rochester showed to his boss. It's a tribute to both actors that they complemented each other so artfully. As the cultural historian Donald Bogle has pointed out, Benny and Rochester were TV's original odd couple, Benny "uptight and tight-fisted," Rochester "loose and at ease with himself and the world."

Benny surrounded himself with other supporting players—I'm not going to get bogged down in rattling them off; you either know Dennis Day from Don Wilson or you don't—but the essence of Benny's appeal is his modernity. Like George Burns and Gracie Allen, he played a version of himself on television, but as the years went on, Benny's image was a subtly more put-upon man, increasingly disrespected by his costars, a man reduced to a blank face, imploring the camera—and by extension, the home audience—to feel some affection for the stingy, petty, peevish man he'd become in public. Affection? Who couldn't love a brave, courtly, self-criticizing fellow like this?

Hate

The "Golden Age" of TV Drama

Have you had a hankering to see *Marty* recently? How about the original TV production of *Twelve Angry Men*? Ever heard of *Patterns*? Of *Thunder on Sycamore Street*?

These are all glowing examples of the so-called "Golden Age" of TV drama—mostly live broadcasts, emanating from studios in New York City, during the the first half of the '50s. TV lore has it that this was a time of remarkable freedom, artistry, and experimentation unequalled in television history. We read the names that emerged from this period—such actors as Paul Newman, Sidney Poitier, Rod Steiger, Kim Stanley; directors on the order of Sidney Lumet, Arthur Penn, and John Frankenheimer; writers like Paddy Chayevsky, Gore Vidal, and Rod Serling. We're supposed to be awed and wistful for a time when television offered quality material: original plays, every week, right in our living rooms.

In fact, most of these plays were mediocre kitchen-sink drama, and the golden age was a tiny moment in TV history—roughly 1953 to 1955. One fundamental tenet of this golden age is that the live production of teleplays was a higher good, that showcases for original TV plays like *Kraft Television Theater, Studio One, Omnibus*, and *Playhouse 90* should have lasted longer for the sake of mass culture.

Yet like everything else about the bastard creature that is television,'50s drama was from the start a compromised endeavor, full of high-minded principles tempered by cynical commercial compromises and spotty execution. Chayevsky's *Marty*, shown on the *Goodyear Television Playhouse* in 1953, is usually cited as the summit of this era's drama. The story of a lonely Bronx butcher, played by a then-little-known Steiger, *Marty* is literally sweaty, in-your-face TV, with director Delbert Mann pushing his camera into Steiger's mug so that we couldn't escape the sad desperation of Marty's bachelorhood. Customers in his shop tell Marty he should be out finding a girlfriend, a wife. The overwhelming pressure on Marty is that he should conform to society's norms, yet Chayevsky—who'd later attack the media for its enslavement of public taste in his satirical 1976 movie script *Network*—doesn't seem to disagree with Marty's customers and the mother with whom the self-described "fat little man" lives: By depicting Marty's solitary misery as utterly bleak—hopeless, despondent, a soul-crushing existence that he might as well end by taking his meat-cleaver to himself—the playwright was ascribing to the most lockstep version of middle-class American values. He settles for a girl his pals describe as "a dog," who was played by Nancy

Marchand (probably best known now as Tony Soprano's grasping mother Olivia).

There's something repellent about the condescension that pervades *Marty*. In many of what are considered the best golden-age dramas, their authors lecture us, stuffing their morals into our heads. Reginald Rose's *Thunder on Sycamore Street* was written as an indictment of racism, about a black family that is ostracized upon moving into a suburban neighborhood. *Studio One*'s sponsor, Westinghouse, complained that Southern audiences wouldn't accept the message that prejudice is bad, and so Rose changed the plot to feature an ex-convict who is shunned by his new neighbors. In this situation, it's hard to know who or what was more insufferable: the cowardly sponsor, the kowtowing author, or *Sycamore Street*'s stick-figure portrayal of human behavior. Rose, a good TV soldier, took back his then–highly acclaimed Nazi-war-crime-trial drama *Judgment at Nuremberg* and erased all references to gas chambers because *Playhouse 90*'s sponsor at that time was the American Gas Association, which didn't cotton to the idea of the public thinking about lethal gas.

One thing that killed the "golden age" was the simultaneous rise of the McCarthy era. Numerous writers, actors, and directors were blacklisted, emptying some of the talent pool. In 1955, for example, *Patterns* carried no director's credit, because it was overseen by suspected-Red Fielder Cook. This is outrageous, certainly, but I'm also not sure that another director, of his own free will, might have wanted to erase his name from Rod Serling's simplistic dramatization of the amorality of the business world. Everett Sloane is a ruthless boss whose ethics threaten to corrupt a young idealist, played by Richard Kiley. Serling later indulged his high-mindedness in some of the more encoded sci-fi and fantasy parables he wrote for *The Twilight Zone.*

By '55, between Joe McCarthy and an industry trend to produce TV shows on Hollywood stage sets, the New York "golden era" had pretty much evaporated. A couple of these teleplays were improved when they were turned into feature films, for example Lumet's artfully shot and tensely edited version of Rose's jury-room jolter *Twelve Angry Men.* For the most part, TV's hallowed time of TV drama retains its luster, because so many of those live productions cannot be seen. It's a legend that would turn to dust if examined closely.

Love

The Most Underrated Live-Action Children's Show Ever: *Ramona*

It was made in Canada. Only about a dozen episodes aired in America. It featured an unknown young actress and was based on a series of children's books that were losing their popularity as the baby-boom turned into Gen X. But *Ramona* (1988–1989) remains an underappreciated treasure on many levels. The American author Beverly Cleary has never attained the sort of sanctioned literary status as, say, Dr. Seuss at one end or Gary Paulsen at the other. But somewhere between Seuss's blithe absurdity and Paulsen's daring naturalism, Cleary created a beautifully self-contained world about the rascally suburban lives of eight-year-old Ramona Quimby, and her bratty older sister Beezus (played by Lori Chodos).

The Canadian TV series, as directed by Randy Bradshaw with many scripts written by Ellis Weiner, a contributor to both *The National Lampoon* and *Sesame Street*, and creator of the snappy, Jason Alexander–voiced 1994 cartoon *Duckman*, was lucky enough to have Sarah Polley play Ramona. Polley, a Toronto native who was nine when she took the title role, was perfect as Ramona, a scraggly haired imp capable of conveying the frustration and bafflement kids feel as they experience embarrassment at school (for example, when poor R. upchucks in class in one startling episode and is comforted by the rare delicacy of a teacher's reaction) or at home, when they outgrow their little-kid status. This was particularly true when Ramona's mom became pregnant and Ramona was no longer the baby of the family.

Since Bradshaw remained gratifyingly faithful to Cleary's books, we get an episode like "Mystery Meal," in which Ramona's mom (Lynda Mason Green) serves the girls tongue for dinner. The sisters are grossed-out ("It's got little bumps!") and object. Mom and Dad (Barry Flatman) suggest that if they don't like the menu, they can cook the next night's dinner themselves. Ramona and Beezus begin the chore resentfully, sniping at each other, but soon get into it, making a joyful mess of the kitchen and serving a not-bad meal. If that doesn't sound exciting, well, that was the point of the *Ramona* series. It took ordinary family events and raised them up for inspection, testing them for stress and elasticity. Life on Klickitat Street is at once idealized and realistic.

Polley went on to play rather more troubled teens in *The Sweet Hereafter, The Hanging Garden* (both 1997), *The Weight of Water* (2000), and fell under the creepy spell of a David Cronenberg shocker, *eXistenZ* (1999), and, further descending into horror hell, was featured in the 2004 remake of *Dawn of the Dead*. She played Sara Stanley in another outstanding children's-lit adaptation, *Road to Avonlea*, in 1990. It's *Ramona* that deserves a revival on DVD, for an innocence heightened by the sharply observed emotional and physical details of family life.

Hate

TV Animals: Eeek!

When it comes to TV animals, I feel much the same way Robert Blake's Baretta did. He took to calling his squawky cockatoo, Fred, "the dummy." "Answer the phone, dummy," he'd sneer, poking fun at the idea of a tough guy like him having a supposedly clever, rather than merely annoying, pet. Blake/Baretta was also speaking for an entire tradition of treating animals as anthropomorphic pals. TV animals tend to fall into two categories: the blandly heroic, forever rescuing their owners—Lassie, Flipper, Rin Tin Tin, Gentle Ben, or Roy Rogers's trusty palomino, Trigger—or the irritatingly cute, forever amusing or exasperating their owners, from *Daktari*'s Clarence, the cross-eyed lion to *Frasier*'s mischievous mutt Eddie. Either way, they came across as either prigs or pains in the ass. The only TV animal I truly admire is one whose greatest fame accrued not from his appearances on a fiction show or a commercial, but a "news" show. On the Dave Garroway–led *Today Show*, the chimpanzee J. Fred Muggs boosted ratings for the initially floundering morning show, annoyed the hell out of Garroway, a man whose fame was founded on his easygoing unflappability, and who was finally whisked off camera for good when he took a good sharp bite out of the plump appendage of a guest, the pleasant musical-comedy and game-show celeb, Peggy Cass, in 1957.

Along television's way, there have also been ridiculous animals, for example *Lost in Space*'s Debby, the space-simian forced to wear a piece of embarrassing, supposedly-futuristic headgear. Another chump-chimp was the star of the campy 1970–1972 series *Lancelot Link, Secret Chimp*, a live-action operative for APE, the "Agency to Prevent Evil." The most interesting thing I learned researching this entry is that the same chimp played both Lancelot and *Lost in Space's* Debby—now *there* was one masochistic, or sadistically agented, monkey. In the TV animal kingdom, as opposed to *Animal Kingdom*, the nature show that spawned ten thousand feeble Marlin Perkins jokes, there was even one fetishistically employed animal— Bruce the ocelot, who used to curl around Anne Francis's fabulous legs and purr with both menace and reflected sexuality in the '60s detective series *Honey West*. *Green Acres's* farm pig, Arnold Ziffel, is included in the same cult of sitcom surrealism of that exceedingly eccentric show.

There's at least one underrated TV animal: Salem the talking cat on *Sabrina the Teenage Witch* (1996–2002). Salem, as voiced by actor-comic Nick Bakay, was a sarcastic little fussbudget with an elaborate wardrobe, dressed in everything from a tuxedo to a bodybuilder's muscle-suit. He undercut the cornball antics of Sabrina with his jaded commentary—he was the Paul Lynde of the cat world, the *Feline Eye for the Supernatural Gal*.

Gotta say, though, Salem was outmatched by the best, and more popular talking four-legger on *Mr. Ed* (1961–1965), a series that holds up surprisingly well, all things considered. All things being the foolishness of the premise—not only does the gabby golden palomino Ed talk, he talks only to his owner, Wilbur, thus setting up the uncountable times Ed tips off Wilbur to some crucial bit of info and Wilbur either tries to coax words from the horse in early editions or fib about his source of knowledge when he knew the animal would remain mum to the world. Credit voice actor Alan "Rocky" Lane for his nicely orotund delivery of even the silliest lines, and Alan Young's underrated performance as Wilbur Post, who could have been just another boob rube but remained a reasonably intelligent man, as befit his character, a big-city architect moved to the country, and the fundamental reason Mr. Ed talked in the first place: Wilbur was the first human he'd encountered out there in the sticks "worth talking to." Would that many humans might adopt the same attitude: Speak only to those worthy of your speech.

Love

The Cartoon That Made *The Point*

Harry Nilsson (1941–1994) was a cult rock 'n' roll figure, an American singer-songwriter whose career was helped considerably by flukes. A hit single he didn't write, Fred Neil's "Everybody's Talkin'," went Top 10 due to its presence in the 1969 film *Midnight Cowboy*. When the Beatles, at a press conference to launch their Apple Records, were asked who their favorite act was, they named Nilsson. It's easy to hear why: Nilsson wrote melodic pop-rock with a psychedelic tinge. He was commercial enough to land a gig writing the theme song for the sitcom version *of The Courtship of Eddie's Father*, "My Best Friend," and his 1971 album *Nilsson Schmilsson* yielded another fluke—a number-one single and *another* song he didn't write: Badfinger's "Without You."

All of which is to explain why a cult artist whose albums consist of 99.9 percent of his own determined whimsy came to write the music and book for a 1971 ABC cartoon special, *The Point*. Simply but prettily animated in a *Yellow Submarine*, watercolor style by director Fred Wolf, *The Point* told the story of Oblio, a little boy with a round head in a fairy-tale kingdom where everybody's head came to a point. Oblio is, literally, pointless. Ostracized for his difference and banished to The Pointless Forest, Oblio and his faithful dog Arrow learn a lesson and return home triumphant: "Everything we ran into had a point—the leaves, the trees . . . so I must have a point, too!"

A simple fable about equality based on a tiresome pun, *The Point* could have been insufferable, but Nilsson made a career of redeeming potentially schlocky sentiments, except when he tried to do it too overtly, on his '73 album of sloshy standards, *A Little Touch of Schmilsson in the Night*. *The Point* was originally narrated by Dustin Hoffman as a father telling his son a bedtime story. *The Point* has a subtle anti-TV message: the kid wants to watch his "favorite program," but Dad insists on telling the story. For whatever reason, when *The Point* was released on VHS tape in 1985, Nilsson asked his pal Ringo Starr to redo Hoffman's vocal performance.

The Point is full of gorgeously gentle, lulling music. "Me and My Arrow" is the best song ever written about a boy and his dog and became a modest hit, and "P.O.V. Waltz" is sneaky psychedelia that includes mention of Nilsson's chief demon, the alcohol that would eventually contribute to his death and mention of which wouldn't make it past TV censors nowadays. Sweet but never sappy, *The Point* is a near-forgotten little remnant of late-counterculture mass-culture outreach whose melodies live on in the back of some of our heads, and, with its release on DVD, may yet happily cloud the minds of future generations as well.

Hate

Bah, Humbug: *A Charlie Brown Christmas*

Charles Schulz's *Peanuts* comic strip was a small masterpiece, a formally innovative work—minimalist yet skilled draftsmanship, kid characters whose adult-world authority figures were never seen, dialogue that partook of the '50s interest in the psychology of what was not said in any given exchange. That Schulz managed to sustain the quality of his strip for half-a-century puts him up there with the geniuses of popular culture. You may think that the guy who sold away the rights to have his creations reproduced on greeting cards, coffee mugs, and what seems like a thousand different items was a cynical sellout. You would be wrong. Schulz gave away a lot of money to good causes, lived a modest life given the enormity of his wealth, and was by all accounts an exceedingly decent human being. If you'd like to freshen your appreciation for Schulz's revolutionary accomplishment (I'm not inflating his importance here—just ask your favorite cartoonist about the influence of Schulz, from *The Far Side*'s Gary Larson to Bill Watterson's *Calvin & Hobbes*—if you can find them), I direct your attention to Fantagraphics Press's monumental ongoing project of releasing every strip Schulz ever drew in annual volumes expected to take more than 12 years to complete.

In the meantime, let me try to persuade you that *A Charlie Brown Christmas*, first airing in 1965, was a dreadful piece of work, mawkish in a way the *Peanuts* strip rarely was, poorly animated and marred by a dreadful "jazz" score. The script by Schulz and producer Bill Melendez contained a rare obviousness: Charlie Brown, put off by the commercialism of the holiday, is searching for the "true meaning" of Christmas. He and Linus, rather than buy the "great big shiny aluminum [Christmas] tree" they started out searching for, end up with a wispy little one—which contains within it that true holiday spirit, of course (because it's *real*, man). Voiced by children in a way that makes you wince at the exaggerated cuteness of authentic voices, and—worst of all—set to Muzak-jazz composed by

Vince Guaraldi, *A Charlie Brown Christmas* was a critical and popular success, winning an Emmy and a Peabody, and only led to more, even worse Charlie Brown cartoon "specials."

The good thing I can say about this drab production is that I'm glad Schulz, a religious man in the best ecumenical tradition, insisted over the objections of the CBS network on retaining some Biblical language in the half-hour: Linus quotes from the King James Bible translation of Luke's description of the Nativity scene. I say this not as a religious man but as someone who thinks if you're going to make a Christmas special, you should feel free enough to put some reference to the Christ child in it, for God's sake.

Love

The Two Most Underrated Shows of the '90s:
Profit and Vengeance Unlimited

And whattaya know: They come from the same guy—writer-producer-creator John McNamara; makes for a tidy entry, no?

No. McNamara is a secret auteur. Other than oil-slick-black humor and a bleak view of humanity, his shows don't share much in common except the sort of venturesomeness that gets you cancelled quickly. *Profit* vanished after four low-rated episodes in 1996. It was a barbed parable about the business mind-set of the decade's booming economy. Adrian Pasdar played Jim Profit, a handsome, square-jawed, polite fellow who joins Grayson & Grayson—G&G, "the fifteenth largest corporation in the world"—where he wants to become president of acquisitions.

Pasdar's Profit narrates his own story in a muzzy, purring voice—his voiceover explains with cold calmness that his ambition will be achieved in the most devious ways possible. Having done devious research, he's able to blackmail a low-level employee into giving him incriminating files about bad business deals in which G&G has or is about to engage. He gets an unwanted visit from a beautiful, if weathered, woman who kisses him passionately, and the hair on your arm raises when Profit delivers the go-to-commercial line after he removes his mouth from hers: "Hi, Mom."

Well, it's his stepmom, but the incest is close enough to make you squirm. I'm pretty sure it was at that point in the premiere that

America decided it wasn't going to take *Profit* to its bosom. During its brief run *Profit* became a secret people told each other: Did you *see* what he did to that guy last night? We also knew from the start that Jim Profit was not only ruthlessly amoral, he also wasn't Jim Profit. He was Bobby Stekowsky, a motherless child abused by his father, raised in a cardboard moving-box with a hole cut into it, and pointed at the television set, so that the only thing our young protagonist saw, morning and night, was the tube. "Reared by TV; imagine that," someone remarks.

John McNamara did imagine it, and *Profit* became the most virulent anti-TV screed ever shown on the television. At the end of every episode, the fully grown Jim Profit stripped naked and stepped into a cardboard box placed in the middle of his apartment. He looked through the hole he'd cut into it at his television set, and slowly went to sleep, dreaming evil thoughts. For years, people passed around the bootlegged, unaired episodes of *Profit* as though they were a kind of pornography, which they were.

Two years later McNamara was back with a *Vengeance Unlimited*, starring Michael Madsen as a kind of bounty hunter of morality called Mr. Chapel. McNamara has a thing for ironic surnames. The gimmick of the show was that Mr. Chapel went around avenging crimes for victims. In return, he asked for one of two things: a million bucks or one favor to be granted to him some time in the future, "no questions asked."

If, say, the episode concerned Mr. Chapel taking on a corrupt fertilizer company whose hazardous-waste ingredients put an innocent little girl on a respirator, Chapel aids the indigent family by calling in a marker on a scientist he's helped previously, who can prove the company's malfeasance. The show was built on a sort of noble ponzi scheme, but I'm making it sound more complicated than it was.

What made *Vengeance* cool was that Madsen was cool in his sharkskin black suits and brilliantined hair. Hulking and imperturbable, he hummed Sinatra tunes and snapped his fingers while pursuing the bad guys. He'd deck a guy with a vicious uppercut, put his hand aside his cheek, and say in mock dainty surprise at his own violence, "Oh, my!" Coming off his brutal role in Quentin Tarantino's *Reservoir Dogs*, Madsen made an exceedingly offbeat leading-man—too offbeat, as it happened, for ABC's audience. The show only lasted three months. But it was a stone gas, a riot—cathartic for those who did tune in, to see Mr. Chapel exact unlimited vengeance on soulless lawyers and obsessed, corrupt IRS agents.

In both series, McNamara was exploring the way power is used in everyday life, particularly in business settings. Both shows were intentionally framed as film-noir thrillers with the protagonists casting long shadows and looming up behind people when they least expected it. Pasdar and Madsen shared deadpan expressions and a remorseless energy, and both spoke in insinuating tones that could be cozy or terrifying. If the running horror-joke of *Profit* was that this psycho executive put his business-shiv between the company's ribs before anyone knew what was happening, an episode of *Vengeance Unlimited* would often end with Chapel telling the favor giver that he or she would never see him again. "Thank God!" they'd exclaim.

He was just too creepy to be a hero, even to those he helped. And *Profit* was just too creepy to be a villain we could root for, like JR on *Dallas* or Richard Hatch on *Survivor*. John McNamara has a fasci-

nating, original take on the way we interact, what our wants and desires are. Too bad not enough people can get on his wavelength.

Hate

The Noah of TV: Steven Bochco Builds the "Arc"

You can quibble about the exact origin of any sort of stylistic innovation, but by industry consent, producer Steven Bochco formalized,
brought to commercial success, and probably invented the "story
arc"—a subplot that plays out over the course of several episodes of
a series—with *Hill Street Blues*. Working with a large ensemble cast
and striving for a verisimiltude that held that not all of his characters' problems or job assignments could be wrapped up each week in
a self-contained hour, Bochco and his writers began developing
longer stories. Trying to locate the middle ground somewhere between your average cop-show episode and the distended storytelling
of soap operas, *Hill Street* was complex enough to make viewers
think they were watching more than a serial melodrama, and gave
them the satisfaction of seeing plots resolve with certain finality.

Pretty soon—after *Hill Street* weathered a low-rated start, won
Emmys, and proved profitable for NBC—other shows began arcing
with varying degress of success, including some subsequent Bochco
productions, most notably *L.A. Law*, very consciously conceived as
the glitzy contrast to *Hill Street*'s gut grit. Producer-writer Stephen J.
Cannell picked up this storytelling technique just as *Hill Street* was
petering out and revitalized it with his own series, *Wiseguy*
(1987–1990). There, Cannell used his supposed hero, Ken Wahl's

FBI undercover agent Vinnie Terranova, as little more than a blank canvas against which his writers might limn portraits of more interesting characters, such as Ray Sharkey's psycho Atlantic City mob boss Sonny Steelgrave over the course of nine episodes, and the greatest arc of them all, Kevin Spacey's Mel Profitt's similarly lengthened mini-odyssey. Spacey has said he owes his career to the genially loopy Profitt character, a philosophy-major drug dealer whose sister, played with glacial inexpressiveness by the beautiful Joan Severance, gave him both drugs that she injected between his toes and sex. No TV series had ever dared raise the subject of incest with such nonchalance—this was decadence unequalled in the medium.

Its critical success and its attraction to producers and writers who felt it was a more creative way to work caused the arc to spawn as many mediocre or bad shows as good ones. *21 Jump Street*, sci-fi shows like *Babylon 5*, the World War II drama *Homefront*, and the ultimate chick-series *Sisters*, all arced as though their lives depended on it, and in most cases, they did. If any of these shows slowed down to tell one coherent story, the banality of the plotting would have stood revealed. Certainly *L.A. Law* alum David E. Kelley ran the method into the ground on his shows *Picket Fences, Chicago Hope, Ally McBeal*, and *The Practice*. Producer Bruce Paltrow had a good initial run with story arcs on *St. Elsewhere* (1982–1988), which featured story lines that included the gradual, convincingly frightening disintegration of Terence Knox's Dr. Peter White from affable yet privately bedevilled doctor to serial rapist after a messy marital breakup. He was ultimately shot and killed by one of the hospital's nurses.

ER really abused the arc storytelling format, stringing along any number of interhospital romances and multiepisode patient subplots that rarely paid off to lasting, transformational effect on the series' regular cast. The same was true of Aaron Sorkin's *West Wing* after its first two glorious seasons. It's now reached the point where any "serious" drama is *expected* to arc—precisely the sort of formula mind-set Bochco was originally trying to break free of. What results are tedious shows like *Third Watch*, the latterday *NYPD Blue* (toward the end of that series, did any of us want to see more of Andy Sipowicz's love life, let alone his backside?), and the promising but botched and over-hyped *Boomtown*, which clung to continuing story-lines that could indeed have been wrapped up in an hour.

In the first few years of the twenty-first century, it was turnabout time, as hits like the *Law & Order* and *CSI* franchises, combined with the economics of the industry, more or less sunk the arc. Story-arcs don't rerun well to large audiences in syndication. Mind you, I'm not talking about series like *The Sopranos* or *Six Feet Under*, whose short seasons preclude the *need* for story arcs—they tell their stories and wrap up production until the next season. Until someone comes along to dredge up the arc, fill in the holes and set it aright again, I say: good riddance.

Love

Richard Hatch Goes Nude on the First *Survivor*

Richard Hatch, the first *Survivor* winner, was a thirty-eight-year-old corporate trainer, openly gay and even more openly egotistical and competitive. Hatch came into the game cocky—"as a corporate trainer, I'm faced with twenty to fifty people in a room at a time that I have to size up very quicky"—and ended up showing his cock . . . and his rear end, to the cameras when he decided to spend most of his thirty-eighth birthday on the Borneo island au naturel. If Hatch had already become the show's most intriguing character for his straight-into-the-camera admissions of lying and strategizing, if he had won over the crusty homophobe Rudy by displaying uncommon skill at spearing fish and providing food for his "tribe," the Tagi, Hatch's casual nudity confirmed his brief central position as the man America loved/hated/feared but most of all—to the surprise of many of the people who felt this way—*wanted him to win*. As moral and moralistic as this country likes to present itself in opinion polls, the nation always falls in love with the con, the con man, the trickster-loner who turns the tables on the group, the mass. We are a country of self-invented individuals, and Richard Hatch was our flabby-assed, private-parts-pixilated representative. Hatch's tropical flashing, about as spontaneous as the "alliances" he concocted as a strategy to screw over his island competitors, was a carefully planned act designed to make himself the one guy no one—the contestants, the camera crew, the home audience—could dismiss. It was the first time since 1974, when the David Niven–hosted Oscar Awards were "streaked" by a prankster, that nudity in a "real" setting, in front of such a large audience, became a topic of national conversation. Yet all Hatch had done, really, was offer a bit of skin that provided film clips as innocent, basically, as a '50s nudist-camp documentary.

Producer Mark Burnett (who'd done a harsher, less playful, more athletic version of *Survivor* for a few years before with *Eco-Challenge* on cable) invented the medium's newest genre—reality-TV—when he cooked up a competition he described as "*Gilligan's Island meets Lord of the Flies meets Ten Little Indians meets The Real World,*" as accurate and succinct a summation for *Survivor*'s irresistible quality as any when it premiered in the summer of 2000. Like most new formats, the show was greeted first as a gimmick with no small amount of derision by TV critics and civilian snobs, the most obvious and irrelevant criticism being that this wasn't really "reality." Gee, no kiddin'. It was an event, a contest, carefully designed as an elaborate outdoor game-show with a million-dollar prize, and any interaction between its participants was constantly mediated by the presence of cameras and the host, the genial, gently-probing Jeff Probst. (Hatch returned in the 2003–2004 "all-star" edition of *Survivor*, and was quickly voted off—his jig was up; he was too much of an obvious threat, but he also provided that series' most cogent comments about game strategy.)

The first *Survivor* is chiefly remembered for its novelty and its "tribal council" tantrum by ousted contestant Susan Hawk. Most of all it's remembered for Hatch, in private life a gay dad. He said that "being gay is the main reason for my success," that his sexual orientation had forced him, over the years, "to interact assertively with people regardless of how they might misperceive who I am or what my motives are."

Well, misperception followed by enlightenment is a crucial pleasure to the process of watching anything new and different on TV. That, and the forbidden thrill of seeing anyone drop his drawers on network television, the last place in pop culture where such a thing is considered taboo.

Hate

Giving Gay a Bad Name: *Queer As Folk* (the U.S. Version, Showtime) and *Queer Eye for the Straight Guy* (Bravo and NBC)

In 1999, British TV's miniseries *Queer As Folk* created by writer Russell T. Davies, presented a marvelously funny, anguished, emotionally complex nighttime soap opera about the lives of gay men in England. The series—which took its name from a Yorkshire proverb, "There's nought so queer as folk," meaning, roughly, a Jim Morrisonism:"People are strange"—demonstrated with tremendous energy and gritty wit that homosexuals are not strange but as needy, horny, funny, dumb, lovable, selfish, and anguished as any comparable group of heterosexuals. Except the gay guys' stomachs were much flatter. *Folk*'s central rake, played by the rouguishly beguiling Aiden Gillen, steamed up Britain's Channel 4 by having sex with a fifteen-year-old boy in the opening hour; the shock effect was intentional: a wittily artful tease which said, in effect, "You think this is going to be titillating? It is, but it's also going to be much more than that, and you'll not be able to resist these randy Manchester blokes if you come along for the ride."

In 2000, Showtime adapted *Folk* and didn't merely ruin it, they effectively prevented America from ever seeing the original. The Showtime reworking of the same chartacters and plot-lines put groaner puns in place of wit, a fudged age for the teen seduced by the rake, Sharon Gless twenty years too late in making overt the sub-text of *Cagney and Lacey* (that the show was about a couple of smart, companionable dykes), and was produced by some of the same folks who brought you the NBC sappy sudser *Sisters* and wrote a brave, earnest but terribly sentimental and melodramatic TV movie about AIDS, *An Early Frost*. It was enough of a success to run for five sea-sons. Unfortunately, the logic of television obviates the need to air the original, British version. As well-intentioned as it is, the U.S. *Queer As Folk* is junky product; the British version is nourishing art. We are the poorer for not having it shown widely in this country.

The "queering" of cable continued with 2003's debut of *Queer Eye for the Straight Guy*. Let's put it this way: How cutting-edge, how daring, how queer-political can a series be if my mother-in-law, who'd never allow Carson Kressley into her house, loves it? The reality-show premise was that the so-called Fab Five gay team in-vades the life of a hapless straight man, redecorates the straight's home and his body (moisturize, mosturize!), and then delivers him to his girlfriend/wife/colleagues a cleaner, spiffer, better man.

The first couple of seasons of *Will & Grace* were more outrageous than *Queer Eye: W&G* was on a major network and yet was even more eager to transgress the TV-accepted boundaries of sexual roles. People watched *Queer Eye* initially because its title was so flagrantly daring and because it premiered on stodgy old Bravo network and therefore felt like a show that had snuck in under the mass-media radar. *Queer Eye* domesticated gay male images for straight America, neutering them in the process. As series television, it was tedious: Seen the first time, it was possibly cute; after more than one edition, it was a repetitive bore.

Love

**Not Dead and Not Forgotten: This Is the Story of
Johnny Rotten . . . on American TV**

One reason England's John Lydon got into the pop music business
was to knock the stuffing out of complacent mainstream culture,
and he was afforded two significant opportunities for this Stateside.
On a May 1980 edition of Dick Clark's *American Bandstand*, the
host sat cozily amongst his teen audience and with his usual bizzer
aplomb introduced Lydon's post–Sex Pistols band Public Image Ltd.
It was standard-operating-procedure to lip-synch one's hit while the
teen audience danced, but Lydon and PiL immediately broke with
tradition and home-audience illusion by declining to sing along with
the lyrics to the reggae-drone "Poptones." This itself was a highly
unusual piece of music for *Bandstand*, for which I suppose we must
give Clark, also the series' producer, some credit for even permitting
on his air.

Lydon sat on the lip of the stage, refusing to move his mouth to
the lyrics, and eventually ambled into the bleachered audience,
inviting—nay, ordering—the kids to get up and lurch around to the
atypical *Bandstand* beat. No such luck, but Lydon and Co. did suc-
ceed in making Clark lose momentary control of the proceedings.
Publicizing the fortieth anniversary of *Bandstand* in 1997, Clark
was asked what the worst moment of the series had been; he quickly
replied that it was PiL's performance.

One month later, on Tom Snyder's regressively present-tense

Tomorrow show, Lydon and bandmate Keith Levine glared balefully at the host, who asked, "Why do you dislike rock 'n' roll so much?" Lydon replied, "It's dead. It's a disease. It's a plague. It's been going on for too long. It's history. It's vile. It's not achieving anything, it's just regression. They play rock 'n' roll at airports. It's too limited." Snyder tried to interrupt—"But there was a time when you didn't feel that way?"—to no avail: "It is too much like a structure, a church," snarled Lydon. "A religion. A farce." Things went downhill from there—from Snyder's point of view, anyway. Having coaxed a cigarette from the puffing host, Lydon continued to badger Snyder even when the latter tried to announce a commercial break. "Excuse me for talking while you're interrupting," Snyder said sarcastically. "Humor me," snapped Lydon. "Not for long," said Snyder. But he did, for another full segment. Snyder may not have "gotten" Lydon and PiL. However, Snyder did know—even in the moment—great TV when it was being taped.

Hate

Howard Stern: Not the King of This Medium

On the radio, Stern is misperceived as a "shock jock"—what he really is, is a social commentator without the niceties that used to bedeck such a title. Stern's vulgar rampages—initially about the hypocrisies of our sexual politics but in the early years of the twenty-first century expanding to take on every sort of politics after he started getting fined by Michael Powell's FCC for "indecent" speech—are righteous and left-leaning. This is true even when he talks a right-wing game to keep his blue-collar listenership from being discomfited. And as a dissector, an exploder, of the conventional celebrity interview, he is an utter original: By setting himself up as the guy you want to be humiliated by, stars traipse into his recording studio to be asked questions far beyond latest-movie/TV-show plugola, delving deep into the fetid psyche of stardom.

Have I set up the essentially sympathetic angle from which I approach Stern? Good, because now comes the bad news: The guy is terrible on TV. His New York–based WOR-plus-affiliates show in the early '90s was a sloppy disgrace, full of lame sight gags and semi-improvised sketches that betrayed Stern and his crew's inability to craft a TV show and maintain the quality of his daily radio show simultaneously. Stern was always funnier complaining about that workload on the radio than he ever was on the TV show itself. His 1994 pay-per-view New Year's Eve special was a creepy travesty, with the self-proclaimed "King of All Media" entering on a toilet and summoning up a succession of tableaux featuring not merely naked women—a Stern given, his unbridled libido is a source of great emotional humor and a destructive force that wrecked his long marriage—but painfully ridiculed and humiliated women, many of whom didn't seem to realize they were there to have contempt heaped upon them, not ogling admiration.

Stern is deeply insecure about his appearance. He drapes his face in long hair and is rarely seen without sunglasses. He obsesses about his weight. On the radio, he realized early on that his hawklike angularity didn't matter—his braying voice was his beauty. On-camera, Stern's insecurities find their outward expression in a ramped-up meanness—he belittles others to draw attention away from himself, which dilutes his humor drastically.

The worst move Stern ever made was permitting the E! cable channel to let cameras into his radio warren in 1994. Stern thought he'd figured out an easy way to extend his all-media kingdom. In fact, he became the emperor without clothes, even though he was the clothed one ordering others to disrobe. *The Howard Stern Show* became, over the morning radio airwaves and then shown late at night on E!, a tiresome procession of vacuous women and men eager to doff their dresses and pants, a clinical experiment in the study of who were more alienated from their own flesh, the host or his guests.

Stern also executive-produced a sitcom for the FX channel in 2000—a parody of *Baywatch* called *Son of the Beach*—that served mainly as a vehicle for the talent of writer-star Tim Stack, perfect as a sweaty, balding, middle-aged lifeguard who radiated desperation. The series itself was just *Benny Hill on the Beach*—lots of big-breast jokes and double-entendre dialogue and slapstick.

Stern should stick solely to radio, where his influence is vast and good. His threat to move to satellite radio in the wake of FCC harassment would marginalize him as a cult artist, which would be a tragedy, because if anyone has ever embodied the term "popular culture," it's Stern.

Love

Homer Simpson's Alcoholism: "And Malt Does More Than Milton Can/To Justify God's Ways to Man"

That *The Simpsons* is one of the medium's greatest achievements is unassailable. The critic Robert Christgau once wrote that unless we accept that the concept of "the great artist" includes "Chuck Berry as well as Marcel Proust, we might as well trash it altogether," and I feel the same way about *The Simpsons* as great art—not just great popular culture. The show has also inspired the closest, most obsessive interpretive readings of any television series. And, no, I'm not forgetting *The X-Files* or *Buffy*.

I've chosen one recurring theme in *The Simpsons*, whose potential for misunderstanding is great. One of the most oft-quoted lines in *Simpsons* history is Homer's toast, "To alcohol! The cause of, and solution to, all of life's problems!" I have seen and heard this line lauded by party revelers and AA members; as with the best writing, it's open to multiple interpretations. Certainly *The Simpsons*'s ongoing use of the Duff beer brand is primarily a critique of corporate alcohol advertising and meant to be abrasively cynical. And Moe, the owner of Moe's Tavern, is the show's most delicately pathetic character—a grouchy, friendless, lonely man who frequently talks about, and has attempted, suicide on more than one occasion. I suppose you could associate his profession—all those years of mopping up after drunks like Barney, who in the 1999–2000 season went sober and transferred his addiction to caffeine.

Homer, however, is an unreconstructed alky, let us not mince words. He drinks to excess and allows it to interfere with his home life: "Marge, send the kids to the neighbors; I'm coming home loaded." He lives in cheerful nondenial. "Alcohol is my way of life, and I aim to keep it." He struggles with his inner demon: "All right, brain, I don't like you and you don't like me—so let's just do this and I'll get back to killing you with beer!" Well, *sort of* struggles. His drinking has had an impact on the real world: The Associated Press reported in 2001 that a thirty-six-year-old British citizen was stopped by police for drunk driving and gave his name as "Homer Simpson." His real name was Peter Simpson. Need I say more, other than to quote this irresistible comment made by the man's lawyer—"The police seemed to have a complete sense of humour failure"?

Wife Marge, whose job it is to have a complete sense of humour failure when it comes to the welfare of her family, has in the past demanded he stop drinking, and Homer has refused. The show's writers may make patently silly jokes about Homer's love of the suds, having him tell Bart, for instance, "Son, when you participate in sporting events, it's not whether you win or lose. It's how drunk you get." But I swear, if you watch *The Simpsons* year in and year out—and who among us does not?—what comes across is, as loath as *Simpsons* staffers are to admit social usefulness, the most depressing portrait of living under the thrall of drunkenness this side of fiery-tongued temperance-advocate Reverend Billy Sunday's turn-of-the-century fulmination: "Listen! Seventy-five percent of our idiots come from intemperate parents; eighty percent of the paupers, eighty-two percent of the crime is committed by men under the influence of liquor; ninety percent of the adult criminals are whisky-made."* Less sentimental than Ray Milland in *The Lost Weekend*, less florid than Jack Lemmon in *The Days of Wine and Roses*, Homer is a walking advertisement for sobriety in a series that despises advertising. It is from a myriad of glorious contradictions such as this that *The Simpsons* achieves exaltation. Oh, and that Billy Sunday speech would sound really good shoehorned into an episode, preferably coming from Homer on a bender.

Hate

Unearned Irony: The Rise and Deflation of Wiseass Humor, from *Mystery Science Theater 3000* to *Family Guy*

Television was commenting on television since the medium was a whippersnapper—George Burns, Jack Benny, and Ernie Kovacs saw to that. But Gen X, who'd been absorbing tube-feeding in utero, tended to deal with everything in the present tense. Any sense of history was Squaresville. When the '80s rolled around, the raft of twentysomethings' take on it, the "Gawrsh, TV's so *stupid*, it's *funny!*" attitude, compelled them to look at everything old as camp. Their approach was and remains howlingly unoriginal, but try telling them that; they're too busy snickering at their own clever sarcasm about anything that passes in front of their small but increasingly bigger screens.

Thus was born, in a 1988 Minnesota UHF station, *Mystery Science Theater 3000*, a cheap way to goof on old movies by doing what

---

*http:/www.reconsider.org/issues/pleasure_drugs_and_classical_vir.htm

young twerps have always done—made sniggering comments on anything that strikes them as silly, serious, or outside their narrow frame of cultural reference. Creator Joel Hudgson was a low-key, wry comedian who invented the set-up: Joel played a low-level stooge on a spaceship who was forced to watch bad movies every week with only the companionship of robots Tom Servo (voiced by Kevin Murphy) and Crow T. Robot (Trace Beaulieau, followed by Bill Corbett in 1997).

You could see their outlined figures along the bottom of the screen as the trio sat through the likes of *The Amazing Colossal Man* and the Joe Don Baker actioner *Mitchell.* They threw comments at the screen like popcorn, stream-of-conscious japery: when a film cuts to a speeding police car, one of the *MST3K*ers hoots, "Meanwhile, on an *Adam-12* episode airing not far away . . ." If a chalk outline of a dead body appears on the screen, it's met with the quip, "Keith Haring was here." By mixing references low and high (and the "high" stuff carried a strong whiff of the secondhand, as though learned by reading *Time* magazine rather than through any firsthand knowledge or interest), *MST3K* pandered to its viewership. See, we're smarter than anything in front of us, the show said. Feh. The show moved to a bigger audience on the Comedy Channel (the soon-to-be Comedy Central), and Hodgson was a pretty amiable host, but his successor in 1993, Mike Nelson, was a stiff yakker who showed how thin this joke could wear. Didn't stop *MST3K* from developing a passionate following that prided itself on picking up on all the pseudo-outre yuks.

The year *MST3K* finally ended, *Family Guy* premiered, on Fox. That and the cheesy ironic attitude was about all they had in common, though. *Family Guy* was creator Seth MacFarlane's take on *The*

Simpsons, which seemed to be: create a cartoon clan but extract the wit. He also thieved from any live-action family sitcom you can name—but made his jokes more vulgar and ham-fistedly surreal. Fox apparently thought a show about a stupid father, a bland mother, a little baby that spoke with an unexplained British accent and plotted to kill his parents, plus an alcoholic pet dog was just the thing to follow Homer Simpson and the gang. But America did itself proud by proving the network wrong. MacFarlane was another Gen Xer hot-wired to believe that merely dropping the name of an author or film director into an episode qualified as some sort of satirical commentary. It didn't.

Fox moved the show a lot before cancelling it in 2002, but the show began airing in reruns on Comedy Central and then sold over a million copies on DVD, reviving this ugly-looking, ugly-minded little speck of post-adolescent piffle. New *Guy* episodes are being produced as I write, and in 2005 MacFarlane plans to introduce a *Guy* variation, *American Dad*, which looks to take the same contemptible point of view that everything in life is crap to be ridiculed. *Family Guy*, like *Mystery Science Theater*, is self-congratulatory TV. While neither will ever attract the mass audience that this mass medium demands, their sizable cults keep them alive in the memories of a few million. Until the next generation comes along, and either sees these shows as the superficial stroke shows they were, or more likely forgets they existed and invents a new slew of "Gawrsh, TV's so *stupid*, it's *funny*" shows. No, ironists: *you're* stupid; TV is, as usual, one step ahead of you.

Love

Pee-Wee's Playhouse as an Edenic Neverland

Far more than just superlative children's programming, *Pee-wee's Playhouse* (1986–1991) is one of the greatest television shows in the history of the medium. Paul Reubens took the infantile-wiseacre character he developed as part of the Groundlings comedy-improv group—part early Jerry Lewis; part Joe Besser's overgrown child "Stinky" circa *The Abbott and Costello Show*—and brought together disparate elements of Los Angeles talent. The *art brut* cartoonist Gary Panter, an underground artist whose posters and album covers had done much to convey the foaming energy of L.A.'s post-punk scene, designed the sets; the avant-prankster musicians the Residents supplied the music. Actors like Lawrence Fishburne was drawling, fringed Cowboy Curtis; S. Epatha Merkerson, later the cop boss on *Law & Order*, was Reba the Mail Lady. The late John Paragon, a marvelous writer, was Jambi, the disembodied-head genie-in-a-box.

Reubens and his collaborators bestowed a precious gift. They created an alternate universe where inanimate objects like a globe, a clock, and flowers spoke. Harking back to TV history, they had the grandiloquent King of Cartoons enter to announce the screening of a brief, ancient, black-and-white cartoon. Reubens even reinstated the old kid-show chestnut of having a "secret word." Every episode, the word was announced at the top of the show—"watch," for example—and whenever a visitor to Pee-wee's house unwittingly uttered it in conversation ("You'd better *watch* out!"), everyone cheered and yelled and sirens went off in happy cacophony.

Reubens taught by example, making sure that everyone spoke in precise grammar. When, in the 1987 "Pajama Party" episode, Fishburne's Cowboy Curtis asked if he could sleep outside under the stars, like a proper cowboy would, he asked, "May I?" "Yes, you may," said host Pee-wee politely. There was always an adult subtext for grown-ups to pick up on if they so chose—images and jokes from gay and punk culture including the impossibly teased-hair of Lynne Stewart's "beautiful" Miss Yvonne and the genie Jambi's wryly gay sarcasm about some of Pee-wee's wishes.

That pajama-party episode can now be seen as a playhouse of innocence now lost: The paradise that became corrupted by the fucked-up sexual scandals that befell Reubens. CBS cancelled the show after the actor was caught masturbating in a Florida adult theater in '91. More startlingly in hindsight, the *Playhouse* and the pajama party echo Michael Jackson's Neverland nightmare. In the *Playhouse* edition, Pee-wee invites all his friends for a sleep-over. They all arrive dressed for bedtime, except for Miss Yvonne, a proper lady who carries her "hostess pajamas" in a small pink suitcase. When she says she'll change into them later, a bedazzled Pee-wee asks, "Can I watch?" to which Miss Yvonne replies with calm firmness, "Of course not, Pee-wee." Reubens had a gift—perhaps now a curse—for remembering the way children ask blunt questions without editing their ids.

No one could do what Reubens did again, and I'm not just talking about his harmlessly naughty byplay. No network would pony up the money for a Saturday-morning live-action series as elaborate as *Playhouse* was. Today, the suits shove cheap, overseas-produced, dubbed animation down kids' brain-stems on Saturday mornings. And Reubens has been robbed of a career on the basis of what is now obviously the most puritanical censure. Atty. General John Ashcroft is likely the only fool in America who'd still say Reubens deserved to be prosecuted.

As I write this, *Pee-wee's Playhouse* is buried treasure. You can't find it on DVD, but videocasettes can be located on the Internet, for too much money. I wish I would say a secret word that would let all hell break loose and reinsert this small masterpiece back into the culture.

Hate

The FCC: Federal Communications Commission, or Fat Cat Coddlers?

A bully pulpit frequently occupied by bluenosed philistines, the FCC almost invariably works against the best interests of the public. Whether it's chairman Michael Powell inveighing against Justin Timberlake's use of the 2004 Super Bowl half-time period to perform a breast examination upon Janet Jackson or the long-term, willy-nilly deregulation of the broadcast industry by one of his predecessors, Mark S. Fowler, the FCC can be counted on to get exercised about the wrong things and to do its best to create a chilling effect on anything daring or adventurous or, let's face it, vulgar. And I write that as a fan of well-executed vulgarity, be it *South Park* or Howard Stern.

Put in place by President Franklin D. Roosevelt soon after he took office, the FCC has a disgraceful history of caving in to government pressure and big business. During the McCarthy era, Pres. Eisenhower appointed a Joe McCarthy protege, John C. Doerfer, to head the Commission; he promptly began harassing TV and radio stations that—get this—weren't carrying McCarthy's campaign speeches. The FCC, which grants licenses to TV stations, went after one of McCarthy's prime targets, Edward Lamb, who owned stations in the South and the Midwest. Doerfer lent the Commission's credibility to McCarthy's charges that Lamb was a communist and had the FCC ask Lamb if he had "girl trouble"—that is, whether Lamb slept around. Classy outfit, eh?

While presidents and politicians both Democratic and Republican have manipulated the FCC to their own ends, the only decent FCC chairman seems to have been Newton "Vast Wasteland" Minnow, appointed by John F. Kennedy. He was an avowed champion of government and broadcast-industry support for noncommercial television as a haven for alternative opinions and programming. Antimonopoly and pro-educational television, Minnow was a whale of a chairman. Post-Minnow, though, the FCC reverted to its crass, cowed and cowardly ways. *The Washington Post* quoted David Levy, director of the Caucus for Producers, Writers and Directors in Hollywood as saying of Fowler's reign during the Reagan administration, "We view his years on the FCC as a disaster for the public good and a gigantic windfall for private interests."

During the Clinton administration, Veep Al Gore urged what Bob Dole called "the billion-dollar giveaway"—that part of the 1996 Federal Communicatuions Act that enabled the FCC under Reed Hundt to give away vast amounts of the broadcast spectrum to the big broadcasting companies under the guise of making the move from analog to digital transmission of TV signals. You think this is mumbo-jumbo? One immediate effect was to enable cable companies to dump low-rated but invaluable networks like CSPAN in favor of whatever crappy network might pay the cable companies more dough to occupy that space, and the "public interest"—which is, after all, the founding mandate of the FCC—be damned.

Thus we come to such present-day spectacles as Michael Powell promising to crack down on "indecency," for example U2's Bono saying "fuck" during NBC's 2003 broadcast of the Golden Globes Awards ceremony. Really, were you or your family marred by Bono's inadvertantly expressed enthusiasm? Shouldn't the FCC have better, more higher-minded things on its mind, like helping vast portions of the country to be exposed to interesting news, commentary, and (both high-cult and low-) arts performances via its founding mission to improve the airwaves not for a few bluenoses and business moguls, but for you and me.

Hey, FCC: go to hell.

Love

Schlock Forgotton: *Silk Stalkings*

Silk Stalkings debuted in 1991 as part of CBS's late-night "Crime-time After Primetime" slate of adventure shows as well as on the USA Network. The idea was that, since it aired when the kiddies were theoretically tucked into bed, *Stalkings* could be naughtier than prime-time fare. The show, created by TV vet Stephen J. Cannell (*The A-Team*, *The Rockford Files*), quickly established its formula. In the opening moments, a murder is committed in a setting that allows for the inclusion of mostly undressed attractive people—in a pool, at a strip club, at a party where two guys snort coke off the rippled belly of a bikini-clad woman. *Stalkings* had a million variations on this. Then our protagonists swagger around the crime scene, interview the now barely dressed attractive people, and solve the crime.

The appeal of *Stalkings* was in how it combined high skin-quotient with soap opera subtext—the evolving relationship between Chris Lorenzo (Rob Estes) and Rita Lee Vance (the too-good-to-be-true-named Mitzi Kapture). Their *Stalkings* was *Moonlighting* crossed with *McMillan and Wife*, but with more underwear. The series captured a late-80s, early-90s tackiness as perfectly as anything VH1 would later peddle as nostalgia. By the end of 1995, Chris and Rita had become lovers, then got married, then Rita got pregnant, then Chris was fatally shot, then Rita decided to leave the force. These story lines drove *Stalkings* to its highest ratings ever. Estes and Kapture had a nice, relaxed chemistry. Estes, the real-life husband of

Melrose Place's Josie Bissett, was charming for a guy whose natural facial expression was slack-jawed, and Kapture was actually a good actress, her sparkly eyes giving off a glint of good-natured self-awareness. *Stalkings* also featured one of the more likable stock police-captain bosses: Charlie Brill as Cap. Doddering boomers may remember him as half of the husband-and-wife comedy team Brill and McCall—McCall being his wife, Mitzi—who made frequent appearances on *The Ed Sullivan Show.*

In later episodes, you could tell the duo was getting a bit bored with the formula, and the pair did everything but roll their eyes on-camera whenever the show wheeled out another girl-in-a-garter-belt subplot. In its fifth season, *Silk Stalkings* underwent drastic cast changes. Chris and Rita were written out of the show, and two new police heroes—Nick Kokotakis's Michael Price and Tyler Layton's Holly Rawlins—replaced them. This switch had the Internet abuzz with *Stalkings* fans who felt betrayed whenever they weren't busy being mean and bitter. Sample postings: "I agree that Price looks like a Neanderthal"; "[Holly] shows too much teeth, anyone else agree?"

Cap had to play stern father figure to Michael and Holly, more callow cops, and they proved to be a couple of drips. Kokotakis mumbled lines through a mouth surrounded by Don Johnston–style stubble; Layton let her acting be done by her hairdo, a Jennifer Aniston feather-cut with blonder highlights, and her wardrobe (hey, detective, wanna bend over that corpse again?). As far as the Internet tooth debate went, I came down squarely: I kinda liked Layton's wide smile.

Always a series for horny insomniacs and lonely people looking for bad fashion tips, *Silk Stalkings* is certainly one of the lesser credits on Stephen J. Cannell's resume, but it captured its moment perfectly.

Hate

The Rise and Fall of *The West Wing*

When it began its run in 1999, *The West Wing* possessed a crackling excitement, a beguiling allure in a genre that was notorious for flopping on TV. The last show about a U.S. president that lasted a full season, let alone won Emmys? That would be . . . none. Never. Thanks to creator-writer Aaron Sorkin's chops as a stage playwright, his lightning-fast dialogue was exhilarating in a prime-time that was increasingly filled with the awkward mumbles of "reality" contestants and hour-long dramas locked into the pseudo-documentary style that Steven Bochco had borrowed two decades before from Alan and Susan Raymond's bona fide doc, *The Police Tapes*.

In bringing to full bloom Martin Sheen, an older actor we'd always kinda liked but had never seen as presidential timber, and surrounding him with a bunch of unknowns and semi-familiar faces who suddenly popped onscreen as the sort of smart, caring people we'd always wished were running the country: that Toby—what an eloquent curmudgeon; that C. J.—what a cool, horsey woman riding herd over the Washington press corps; that Sam Seaborn—what a . . . what a Rob Lowe! *The West Wing* was a small miracle. A drama about politics that made you laugh—every week a little play that taught lessons in civics and civility—gee, Sheen's President Josiah Bartlet spoke Latin, and he wasn't stuck-up about it at all! And 99.9 percent of it was the vision of one man, Sorkin: See, TV could be the medium of solo auteurism!

Boy, did *that* not last long enough. By the start of season three, Sorkin's strain was showing. Everybody was still smart and wise-

cracking, but they also *all sounded the same*. The series' signature
shot—the so-called "walk-and-talk"—perfected in collaboration
with producer-director Tommy Schlamme, a method of plot
exposition-delivery that sent characters hurtling down White House
hallways tossing out facts and plot updates . . . all this had become
self-parodic. Like a coke-head or a brilliant student with A.D.D.,
Sorkin couldn't seem to sustain his own interest in the core of regulars and his abiding themes (see civics and civility above). He was introducing and dropping too many characters: Lily Tomlin as a
loony-left-leaning aide to the Prez! And hey, what happened to
Stockard Channing's First Lady for months on end?

The Wing started smelling of desperation, or Sorkin's ego-wrung
perspiration. In its fourth season, the show was still snatching Emmys out of the cold, live hands of *Six Feet Under* creator Alan Ball,
Sorkin's chief competition in status within the industry at that time.
Suddenly the ratings for *West Wing* were in freefall, dropping 20 percent in less than a year—30 percent among the networks' most
prized, 18- to 49-year-old viewers. Part of the reason was competition: the romance-novel-that-moved, *The Bachelor*, was beating *The
Wing*; "reality" had overtaken Sorkin's carefully crafted alternative-
reality, a post-Clinton Democratic presidency with principles and
heartland popularity.

The heartland was bedazzled by *The Bachelor* soap opera, and
Sorkin was resorting to feeble stunts like having Christian Slater
guest-star as a flirtation for Janel Moloney's Donna. A subplot about
a war we formented in fictional Qmar (what, suddenly conserving
your energy by getting stingy with the vowels, Aaron?) was more of a
quagmire than a C-SPAN Pentagon briefing. Lowe bailed out. He'd
always nursed a grudge that the show was originally conceived as a

star vehicle for him, not Sheen. In 2003, Sorkin quit, handing the show over to co-exec-producer John Wells, a capable craftsman who was also guiding the now-only-intermittently-compelling *ER* and the snorer *Third Watch*. *The West Wing* on Wells's watch became nearly unwatchable, a faded Xerox of Sorkin's old sentiments, phrased clumsily by a staff of valiant but hapless impersonator-writers.

The show really did lose ground due to the Bush presidency, but not because the country, as I read many times in reviews, had "turned conservative" or Republican overnight. Rather, it was because Sorkin started writing angry screeds. He rightly resented what he described to me as "the demonization of intellect" that he heard and saw in Bush and his advisors. A hortatory Sorkin is a literal-minded writer, who set up Republicans not as they were, but as boobs, patsies, of affable juggernauts like John Goodman's interim president. The public knew this was a false, condescending view of people, and so even many of those who weren't watching *The Bachelor* withdrew their vote for Bartlet and the *Wing* administration.

Love

Paul Lynde: The Quintessential Querulous Queer Man

The son of a Mount Vernon, Ohio, police chief, Paul Lynde (1926–1982) was the sort of performer who could sell a feeble joke purely on the strength of his delivery. He'd squint until his eyes were merry slits, and open his wide mouth into a toothy, carnivorous smile. He'd hunch his shoulders and give them a pert little shake. Then he'd issue the punchline rapid-fire, often dropping his final consonants in the Midwestern manner.

He was the key "center square" for much of his 1966–1979 tour-of-duty on *Hollywood Squares*:

Host Peter Marshall: Paul, what do you call a man who gives you diamonds and pearls?
Lynde: Darling!

Lynde would follow up the joke with an uproarious cackle. Even if you didn't think his material was funny, he could sell a joke with such extravagant brazenness that you couldn't help chuckle and love him.

Nowadays, we are obsessed by assigning sexual orientation to celebs whose careers were spent declining such assignation. And so, Lynde's talent has been obscured by tales of his off-camera homosexual antics as well as the telltale signs of a life spent unhappily closeted—too much booze and recreational drugs, some combo of which is said to have cause the heart attack that killed him at a mere fifty-six.

Turning Lynde into a gay icon can celebrate his talent in context, but can also minimize his achievement. Starting out in the early '50s as an acerbic stand-up comic who was more sour-puss than cut-up artist, Lynde was a Broadway *Fresh Face of 1952*, and became a stage star in the '63 production of *Bye Bye Birdie*. He did some movies, playing essentially the same character—the caustic queen with a quick mind and whiplash tongue—in schlock like *Beach Blanket Bingo* and *The Glass Bottom Boat*.

TV was his medium of choice, providing the best paycheck and allowing him to use his gifts to redeem mediocre material, whether he was the practical-joke-loving warlock, Uncle Arthur, in a recurring role on *Bewitched*, a guest star in countless sitcoms in the late '60s and the whole of the '70s, or his *Squares* tenure.

Go on the Internet, and you'll find stories about Lynde being fired from *Squares* for drinking on the job—ye gods, who wouldn't need more than a few belts to work with personalities like Abby Dalton and David Brenner?—and letting loose sodden tirades at the host and audience during tapings. Give the guy a break. Lynde was an endlessly amusing, intelligent man whose sexual persona limited his choices in show biz in a way that's tragic and criminal.

Peter Marshall: Paul, can you get an elephant drunk?
Lynde: Yes, but he still won't go up to your apartment!

Someone else undoubtedly wrote that line ("I'm a script man," Lynde once said of his *Squares* tenure), but it was his squinched face, the way he spat out the words as "he still won't go up to ya ap-

arhrt-ment!" that made you laugh. He was queer before queer was cool.

Hate

Roasting Miss Piggy

Don't misunderstand me. Jim Henson was a genius, not a word I use lightly. In the early '50s, he combined revolutionary puppetry with the smart-ass attitude that Edgar Bergen had brought to ventriloquism two decades earlier, and came up with the malleable Muppets. Kermit the frog, like Bugs Bunny and Daffy Duck, is a marvelously obstreperous, anarchic, entirely unsentimental character. Like Maurice Sendak, Henson knew that kids like being scared a little—that it's *good* for them to be unsettled. The truly angry Oscar the Grouch and the alarmingly voracious Cookie Monster, voiced by the future movie director Frank Oz, resulted from this predilection.

Oz also gave voice to Miss Piggy for the first time in 1974. Miss Piggy quickly became the most popular Muppet and the least funny, most obnoxious yet bland, culturally influential of Henson's creations. Initially introduced all too appropriately on a 1974 TV special hosted by bland trumpet mogul Herb "A Taste of Honey" Alpert, Miss Piggy, with her formidable bodice, her showy pastejewelry, and elbow-length opera gloves, was doubtless conceived as Henson's take on Margaret Dumont, the high-society comic foil in the Marx Brothers movies. Like Dumont, Piggy was a figure of fatuity, a snobby pseud. The pink puppet's trilled catchphrase—"*Moi?*"—begged to be ridiculed by the Muppet Groucho, Kermit.

Unfortunately, you, the public, opted to love this pig, to be delighted by her dithering inanities. Miss Piggy was Paris Hilton with a lot more meat on her bones: a rich snot embraced by people she considered her lessers—that is, you.

Soon, decent, ordinary citizens started saying, *"Moi?"* instead of the good old American "Who, me?" as a way of signalling affronted irony. Miss Piggy never really matured into a mistress of irony. Instead, she began, ah, hogging the precincts of Muppetry, from *Sesame Street* to the *Muppet Movies*. The ascent of the imbecilic Miss Piggy was the sole example of a Henson creation overtaking its creator, who died in 1990. Her popularity demanded her pervasiveness, which only increased the limitations of her comic possibilities. Miss Piggy became the literally show-stopping centerpiece of too many Muppet projects. *Moi?* I would like nothing more than to see her roasted on an inverted garbage-can-top platter held aloft by Oscar the Grouch, a rotten apple stuffing her mouth into silence.

Love

The Best Sports Show on TV, Ever: *Pardon the Interruption*

Yes, anything that aired with Howard Cosell in his prime was inescapably good television. I liked ESPN's *SportsCenter* in its early years, around the same time Aaron Sorkin was holed up in a hotel room doing rewrites on *A Few Good Men* and became so enthralled by the intelligent-wiseass style of *SportsCenter*'s anchors that he created a woefully-too-short-lived sitcom based on it, *SportsNight* (1998–2000). *Pardon the Interruption*, however, the daily half-hour ESPN version of *Siskel & Ebert*, which premiered in 2002, is in its way a perfect piece of television—I would go so far as to say, a genius concept flawlessly cast and executed.

The concept: Sportswriters Tony Kornheiser and Michael Wilbon debate sports issues, from big trades to steroids to the relative merits of team mascots. But here's the cool thing, using the medium the way it should be used: a list called the "Rundown" appears along the right side of the screen. It tells you what topics the guys are going to be discussing ("Steroids," "Mascots," etc.) and a clock ticks as they talk. The duo never spends more than two minutes on each subject—if they do, a bell clangs loudly, and they're forced to move to the next item.

This simple idea is genius. Even if *you don't even care* about sports, like me, *PTI* compels you to keep watching, because you can look at the Rundown and say to yourself, "Well, I don't care about steroids, but I wanna hear what they have to say about mascots." The show clutters the screen in a way that is actually helpful, unlike on the all-news channels—it tells you what's coming next and keeps you hooked.

Of course, it helps that the hosts are so amusing. Wilbon is a straight-shooter who, unlike most TV talking heads, never minces words. When the ornery owner of the Cincinnati Reds, Marge Schott died in 2004, Wilbon's summation of the woman who once said, "Hitler was underappreciated" was succinct: "She was vile," he said. Kornheiser is a gifted print humorist, and his braying voice is funny-aggressive rather than annoying—he comes up with more spontaneous one-liners in a week than Jay Leno has done in his entire *Tonight Show* tenure.

Plus the show has a feature I wish the news channels would adopt. Near the end of the show, a researcher, Tony Reali, aka "Stat Boy," comes on camera and corrects the factual errors Wilbon and Kornheiser may have made in the heat of argument. They admit their mistakes! They talk about all of pop culture as well as sports! They bellow at each other, but their rants contain the articulateness of the print-writers they are! This is what great television is about.

Hate

PBS: Public Broadcasting Spinelessness

I almost choked on my guacamole-flavored Dorito chips the other night. Clicking through the dial, I landed on a PBS station running a Jack Paar tribute, which like all such salutes was edited and voice-overed to within an inch of the life it was saluting. (You barely had time to catch the immortal answer the pianist/wit/hypochondriac/ they-don't-make-'em-like-this-anymore Oscar Levant had to Paar's question, "What do you do for exercise?": "I stumble and then I fall over.") Anyway, what made me gasp and inhale dangerously jagged guacamole-chip shards wasn't the sight of Paar—it was the pause in the show to raise funds for PBS. They still have PBS fundraisers! For *what*?

For *Antique Roadshow* and *The Forsyte Saga II*? For the pathetic attempt to piggyback onto reality-TV with *Frontier* and *Colonial Houses*? For offering hack versions of an exhausted *Masterpiece Theatre* and for making sad, multi-culti-pandering versions of Tony Hillerman's fine Native American thrillers for *Mystery!*? These two series, by the way, have been yanked out of their time slots in recent years so blithely that not even my loyal old mother can locate them. You *boobs!* For *This Old House* and whatever variation they can come up with on *The Three Tenors* to nod to high culture and drag it into the middle-brows of what it perceives as its no-brow audience?

I have no sympathy whatsoever for PBS, which has permitted itself to be jerked around by every conservative Administration and every right-wing squawk group that has managed to convince the majority of the TV audience that still even thinks of PBS that public broadcasting should pay its own way, that it should present "all sides of an issue," that it shouldn't do anything that might offend any segment of its ever-aging demographic. You spineless PBS twerps—why didn't you fight back in 1972 when *The Great American Dream Machine*, a sassy current-events anthology featuring the endearing, appallingly forgotten Marshall Efron and a pre–*60 Minutes* Andy Rooney, was allowed to be pushed off the air? Why didn't you say, "Screw you!" to the homophobes who bowdlerized and marginalized the broadcast of the Marlon Riggs AIDS revue *Tongues Untied* in 1991? PBS, why haven't you persisted in reminding your audience and our government that there should be programming that should be funded not by begging for pennies and handing out tote bags while airing *Lawrence Welk Show* reruns, but which should be subsidized—by a tax on TV sets, and a dunning of the commercial networks, blood money for garbage like *Fear Factor*, and the opportunity for us to give a chunk of change out of our income tax?

All this is, I'm afraid, probably too late. There are still a number of reasons we should be grateful for PBS's existence, foremost among them *Frontline*, whose searing documentaries remain provocative and essential. If only for producer Ofra Bikel's magnificently relentless exposures of the loathsome sham Satanism scandals in day-care centers, *Frontline* deserves the combined salaries of the entertainment presidents of CBS, NBC, ABC, Fox, and WB combined, annually unto eternity. Any time Helen Mirren wants to make another *Prime Suspect* up until the moment she drops dead, she should be doing it on PBS. Giving up, acceding to the argument that cable does nature shows and biographies better than you, so why bother trying to compete—that's as moronic as endorsing the fucking purple dinosaur you used to pimp out for donations before Barney-fever subsided.

You've been done grievously wrong by your country, PBS. But you also have yourself to blame. You want a constructive suggestion? Cease production of everything except *Frontline* and Helen Mirren. Sorry, I apologize to my mother-in-law, but I don't see the need for Jim Lehrer anymore. Rerun the best stuff from your better years. Do you realize how much publicity you'd receive, to say nothing of good will, boomer viewership, and $$$, if you just put the original versions of *Dream Machine, The Jewel in the Crown, Danger UXB,* Leonard Bernstein's classical music series for children, Robert Hughes's *The Shock of the New,* and Julia Child back on the air? Don't you have any sense of what you've meant to television history, and how you've disgraced that past?

Love

The Only Person Who Ever Told Bill Cosby to
Fuck Off: Lisa Bonet

In the first few seasons on *The Cosby Show*, Bonet was the gravely beautiful middle daughter of Dr. Cliff Huxtable's TV family, rebellious whenever she wasn't unreadably moody. This was a different kind of sitcom character, and a different kind of black sitcom character: In matters of both genre and race, Bonet's Denise was an original creation, and not because the writers or show-creator Cosby conceived her that way. Bonet's own demure-to-sullen demeanor was only enhanced as she grew older and added funky dreadlocks and a baggy, hippie wardrobe to her onscreen image. When the nineteen-year-old Bonet left the show after three seasons, the ostensible reason was that she'd spun off for her own series, *A Different World*, but she'd also costarred with Mickey Rourke in *Angel Heart*, executing a sex scene (that verb is intentional—screwing Mickey Rourke at that point must have required a bonus in her contract rider) that avoided an X-rating only after careful cuts. This was not the sort of thing the on- and off-camera strict-paternal Cosby wanted his TV daughter doing.

During the mid-'80s, *The Cosby Show* was a huge phenomenon—the show that saved the sitcom format and a good chunk of NBC's fortunes at that point. Bonet's implicit fuck-you to the Cos was unprecedented. She only stayed on *Different World* for its first, 1987–1988 season, then married rock musician Lenny Kravitz and truly left for a different world, accepting acting jobs only sporadically.

Seen now in the syndicated *Cosby Shows*, Bonet's Denise is a throwback to the kind of '60s rebellion that Bill Cosby himself had denied in order to join the white entertainment establishment. He, too, became increasingly serious, sullen, and self-absorbed (off-camera), suggesting he had a lot more in common with the prickly Bonet than he would ever admit. Watch them now for the way their father-daughter sparring is played for laughs but with a jaggedly emotional edge.

Hate

"Tackling" Issues on TV

Any time you see a TV listing or a review telling you a show is going to "tackle" an "issue," run away from your TV set. This is invariably a red-flag to a viewer to avoid like SARS a very-special-episode that raises such controversial subjects as death, abortion, drugs, or sex but never actually takes a stand on the issue, other than to acknowledge it exists, lest the answer offend a sponsor or a significant chunk of the audience. Yet, with maddeningly regularity, the "problem" is resolved within the allotted thirty or sixty minutes of the show's length.

Thus the TVLand cable network's Web site cites *Family Ties* for being "unafraid to tackle tough issues. There were more than a few serious episodes including: the Emmy Award–winning episode "My Name is Alex," a one-man show in which Alex is forced to deal with the death of his best friend who is killed in a car accident, and a three-part episode dealing with Steven's heart attack and bypass surgery. None of these was among that mediocre show's finest moments—they were, instead, typical of what happens when a sitcom goes "tackling": the laughs subside, the soundtrack is filled with sympathetic clucks and moans, and the viewer is bored with actors delivering obvious truths.

Cable TV is a great one for tackling: JENNIFER BEALS TACKLES ISSUES OF RACE, SEXUALITY ON *THE L WORD*, reads a headline on a Web site specializing in lesbian issues (www.afterellen.com): No, *The L Word* revels in issues on race and sexuality, as does FX's "controversial" lathered-up nighttime soap *Nip/Tuck*, a show, one Web fan (www.aaronsw.com) writes, "tackles topics like faith, rape, drugs, suicide, ethics, and sexual identity with such honesty and care that it's hard to believe they got away with it on TV. Lesbians, transgenders, and threesomes are treated as nothing out of the ordinary." Sorry, Aaron SW: *Nip/Tuck* exploits these subjects for thrills, laughs, and shock value, and does it with hack glee.

The Knight-Ridder columnist Jane Eisner praises MTV in 2002 for "depart[ing] from its usual fare of grinding music videos and shrieking, bare-bellied teenagers to present a half-hour news special tackling the issue of sexual education in the schools." When I tuned in, all MTV was dispensing was a lot of stock footage of kids making out on other, broadcast-TV shows and some sensible words about condoms and abstinence. And don't get me started on the number of times the topical-news shows headed by comedians like Bill Maher and Dennis Miller are said to tackle society's ills.

Of course, only the most high-minded of shows can "tackle" the most serious of contemporary tragedies: *SESAME STREET* TO TACKLE SEPTEMBER 11 ISSUES, read another newspaper headline, affixed to a story leading off with: "*Sesame Street* is to tackle issues related to the September 11 attacks. The first episode deals with Elmo's fears after he witnesses a fire that breaks out in a cafe. He has to be comforted by real-life firefighters."*

Really, the only entertainment series I can think of that tackled an issue with forthrightness was *Maude*'s two-part "Maude's Dilemma," in 1972—said dilemma being whether or not to have an abortion. The show's writer, Susan Harris, really did tackle it: she permitted the character to get one. A storm of controversy followed. It's been a rare character indeed—none, I would assert, on network television, and please prove me wrong—who's gotten one since.

So much for TV's record on "tackling" the unpopular. It's not something the medium has the spine to do.

*http://www.newsforthesoul.com/02jan/1-2-streetsesame.htm

Love

The Best Speeches Ever Written for a Guest Star/Coolest Philo Farnsworth Name-Check/Most Subtle Advertisement for Sobriety, All in One Segment: *SportsNight*

William H. Macy was brought onto a few episodes toward the end of Aaron Sorkin's real gift to television, the short-lived *SportsNight* (1998–2000). Macy probably agreed because he's married in real life to costar Felicity Huffman, who played a producer for the show's ESPN-like sports channel. Macy's character was a gun-for-hire, brought in to boost ratings. In the October 19, 1999, episode, a trio of network dweebs-with-power bustle in to give stupid but imperious "notes" to the staff on what must be done, in the process insulting the show-within-the-show's executive producer, Isaac Jaffe, played by Robert Guillaume. Macy, unbeknownst to the staff, which had taken an instant dislike to this unreadable outsider, beckons the dweeb trio to follow him, and unfolds the greatest of Sorkin's "walk-and-talks," those motor-mouthed speeches he patented to greater acclaim on *The West Wing*.

Macy tells the dweeb trio the story of Philo Farnsworth, the inventor of television. As usual, Sorkin could not resist condescension—he telegraphs the message that the dweebs, who owe their livelihoods to TV, don't know who invented it. Macy explains that not only was Farnsworth a visionary, but he had a great brother, *not* a visionary. The brother was a faithful fellow who taught himself to be a glassblower just to create the unique glass tubes needed to create the first television sets. Macy's point is that none of them is fit to tie Farnsworth's shoelaces, and that he himself is much like Farnsworth's brother—not by any stretch a visionary, but a useful functionary.

Then he gets down to brass tacks. Stopping the walk-and-talk, he turns to the tallest, most arrogant dweeb and says with a wide yet chillingly cold smile that if they ever disrespect Isaac again, "I will rededicate the rest of my life to ruining yours. I have absolutely no conscience about these things," he concludes. And he shows the suitably shaken dweebs the door.

Then Macy gathers the *SportsNight* staff and tells them they don't have to like him, but he's here to help them. "I have two priorities; the first is getting from the beginning of the day to the end of the day without having a drink, and the second is to aid you in putting on the best show possible." The staff—the stars of the show—are also, suitably, shaken and left in silence.

This is why God invented VCRs, videotape, TiVos, DVDs, and any other recording devices. Play this over and over for inspiration.

Hate

The Women of *Law & Order*: A Lamentation

These poor women. These poor, underutilized women. These poor, and in some cases, untalented women. These poor, some of them talented, women.

Okay, Kathryn Erbe on *Law & Order: Criminal Intent*, she's really good, but she's doomed to exist in the shadow of that egregious

ham-bone Vincent D'Onofrio. You suspect S. Epatha Merkerson of
the original-flavor *L&O* is really good because maybe you've seen
her in other things, but, let's face it, she was allowed to do more acting as Reba the Mail Lady on *Pee-wee's Playhouse* than delivering the
3,784th variation on "Go check out this guy" order to Jerry Orbach
and whomever he's teamed up with, depending on what rerun you're
watching.

But the rest—these women are poorly served by the *Law & Order* franchise. It's been said that NBC told producer Dick Wolf to
oust Dann Florek from *L&O* in 1993 and replace him with a female boss because the series needed to attract more women. If true,
Merkerson certainly deserved the work . . . it's just that there's so
little of it to do. On the flagship show, it's still pretty much 50 percent track-the-criminals, 50 percent try-'em-and-try-to-fry-'em.
That's where the female assistant district attorneys come in. And
go. Jill Hennessy (1993–1996)—she had to leave to do *Crossing
Jordan* just to prove she was a bad actress; Carey Lowell
(1996–1998)—I'm thinkin', two seasons? probably very little off-
camera chemistry with costar Sam Waterston and the producers,
too much chemistry with boyfriend Richard Gere; Angie Harmon
(1998–2001)—a good-looking person and a wooden actress; and
Elisabeth Röhm (2001–2005)—seems to have been recruited by
Wolf on one of his infrequent visits to a farm. Oh, calm down—I
mean she looks like a healthy farm girl, nothing worse than that.
The only semiregular woman I ever thought did a terrific job on
L&O was Carolyn McCormick's tight-jawed psychiatrist Dr. Elizabeth Olivet (1991–1997), but once again, too little face time, too
much psychobabble substituting for characterization.

Over on *L&O: Special Victims Unit*, I'm not including Mariska Hargitay because she's a costar. In fact, by the no-personal-life-details rule of the *L&O*s, we know too much about her character. Michelle Hurd played a detective for two seasons but was shunted aside for Ice-T's Fin. The big liability on this series was Stephanie March as A.D.A. Alex Cabot, who could occasionally be substituted with a life-size cardboard cut-out in a courtroom scene without anyone being the wiser. March got the most dramatic send-off of anyone on any *L&O* show: in the early episodes of 2003, Cabot got involved in a gangland case and was murdered . . . or so we thought. Turns out she was put in the witness protection program. Why? No reason that made sense, other than the fact that maybe the writers thought killing her off was too old-school. She's been supplanted by Diane Neal's Casey Novak, a chipper woman who has yet to display much in the way of canny law sense because we don't see much of her, except when she's placed in a subordinate role, for example, acting behind guest star Marlo Thomas, as Novak's former mentor.

This brings the circle back to *Criminal Intent*'s Erbe, a fine, understated actress with a puckish sense of humor, none of which is initially apparent when her gigantic costar is busy waving his turkey-sized hands around, and bending his broad frame into odd positions to unnerve suspects and unsuspecting viewers. Erbe manages to give her line readings a wry, *juuuust*-this-side-of-sarcastic twist, signalling to us that she knows she's being upstaged and doesn't really care for it, but what can she do? She's lucky she made it through her real-life maternity leave and still had her job when she came back. A *Law & Order* paycheck is a good gig, and Wolf could have thrown her to the wolves. Maybe some year, when contract negociations with D'Onofrio go sour, and with that moody big bastard, you *know* they will, maybe Dick Wolf will have the guts to fire him, make Erbe the real front-and-center star of the show, and let some pretty-boy actor come in and stand obediently two steps behind Erbe at all times. *That* would be true justice in this criminal justice system . . .

Love

Laverne & Shirley: Lovable & Silly

A spin-off of *Happy Days* that easily surpassed its source in laugh-power, *L&S* (1976–1983) was as authentic a working-class sitcom as more-lauded shows like *The Honeymooners* or *Roseanne*. Well, authentic if you combine the silly saga of two 1950s Milwaukee brewery workers with the slapstick of a lower level with that of The Three Stooges. Future film director Penny Marshall got this job via good old Hollywood nepotism—her brother Garry was the producer of *Happy Days*. Future sad-sack guest star on shows such as *Seventh Heaven* Cindy Williams probably thought this, following her appearance on film in *American Graffiti*, was but a stepping stone to greater stardom.

In both cases, these women have never done anything to surpass the boisterously energetic physical humor and female camaraderie of *Laverne & Shirley*. Marshall's Laverne DeFazio was a variation on the public persona Marshall presented in interviews—querulous, always slightly grumpy, innately suspicious of everyone. Marshall was also the least convincing Italian on TV since Topo Gigio, and her sour-Jewish-tummler sense of humor only enhanced her character. Williams's Shirley Feeney, by inevitable contrast, was all-accepting, gullible, a saucer-eyed innocent. As roommates forever in search of boyfriends, they carried on that air of desperation that Rose Marie's Sally wore like perfume in *The Dick Van Dyke Show*, except that *L&S* probably smelled more than a little like the hops that permeated the factory they labored in all day, and their most persistent would-be suitors were a genius pair of cretins, Lenny (Michael McKean) and Squiggy (David L. Lander). McKean and Lander were both gifted improvisors who seemed to be winging half their break-the-girls'-door-down entrance scenes. McKean had been a *Spinal Tap*per and went on to become part of writer-director-actor Christopher Guest's stock company in films like *Best In Show* and *A Mighty Wind*. Laverne and Shirley were hard-working, always scheming for financial independence and marital dependence. Lenny and Squiggy were blissful idiots absurdly confident of their powers of seduction and worldliness.

The series became cluttered with the increasing prominence of Phil Foster, an old-school comic here reduced just to yelling a lot as Laverne's pizza-parlor-owner father, and the talentless crooner Eddie Mekka, positioned initially as Shirley's boyfriend. The patent lack of chemistry between them only fueled the suspicion that what we were watching between Laverne and Shirley was an encoded, forever-unconsummated lesbian relationship of the most proletarian sort. What gives *L&S* its continued pleasure is not its subtext but its ur-text: the sight of two women throwing themselves against slammed-shut doors, climbing walls in the most unladylike ways, and punching the living daylights out of the prize saps Lenny and Squiggy. These girls were carrying on Lucille Ball's tradition grandly, with less acclaim. But Williams very unwisely decided she was too big a star and started staging walkouts and work stoppages, and the series steadily lost its spurting comic steam. *Laverne & Shirley* holds up as the sort of uncool, un-ironic, unself-conscious fun that a performer like Whoopi Goldberg is incapable of creating.

Hate

Whoopi Goldberg—Bad TV Star in So Many Formats

It's hard to remember now, but there was a brief moment, at the start of her career, when Whoopi Goldberg did something besides play Whoopi Goldberg. She created varied characters—impersonating a little girl, a "surfer chick," and others—and she shaped a one-woman performance that caught the eye of director Mike Nichols, who showcased Goldberg's talent in a 1984 Broadway production that made her a star. She's never looked back—and in her case, that's been her crucial creative flaw. Once Goldberg became a star, and she saw that people laughed hard at her own natural "Aren't I a saucy gal?" attitude, she seemed to figure, why mess with what the masses like? It was easier just to be herself—or an image of herself, tough-talking, cold-staring, slow-burning, lapsing into the black slang of her generation (she's in her late forties) to get quick, thin laughs. Though she's brought a lot of people a lot of pleasure in dodgy film vehicles (my kids used to watch *Sister Act* and *Corrina, Corrina* over and over again on tape), no one would accuse her of living up to her potential.

That's most true of her TV work. Whether hosting the Oscars in 1999 by making jokes in white-face as Queen Elizabeth or resorting to "beaver" puns, or occupying the *New Hollywood Squares* center-square by fiat (she was one of the game show's producers), Goldberg is infuriating: an obviously intelligent, shrewd performer who's decided she'll go for the easy laugh every time out, because the dumb audience doesn't know better anyway.

Whoopi in serene, kindly mode is almost as appalling as rude, bumptious Whoopi. Her 1992–1993 talk show featured one celebrity per night, grilled for a full half hour. At the end of thirty minutes, no guest arose from his or her Whoopi cushion without the assurance that Goldberg felt she has been in the presence of a very, very special person. Questions on *The Whoopi Goldberg Show* had the consistency of Nerf balls, golden Nerf balls lobbed ever so gently, respectfully, at the stars. Goldberg to Elizabeth Taylor: "Has your sense of self come a very long way from that little girl in *National Velvet* to the woman you are now?" Taylor said yes, her self had come a long way. How about Goldberg to Ted Danson?: "I've read that Ted Danson and Sam Malone are very different." Yep, the actor agreed that he is indeed dissimilar to his character on *Cheers*. For example, Danson, unlike Sam, wears scholarly looking horn-rims and says things like, "I think we're ready for a different creative rhythm in our lives," when what he really meant was, "Oh, Lordy, yes, I hope this is *Cheers*'s last season!" And there was Goldberg to Tom Metzger, former Ku Klux Klan leader and head of White Aryan Resistance, or WAR: "So, let me get this straight," said Goldberg softly, "you think nonwhites should be strongly encouraged to have abortions, and whites should not." When Metzger nodded that, yes, this was indeed the way he, the good ol' USA's supreme pointy-headed white racist, felt, Goldberg smiled warmly, said in a low voice, "Somethin' to think about," and cut to a commercial. Somethin' to think about, indeed. But not for too long—*The Whoopi Goldberg Show* was cancelled after one season.

Having bombed in a sitcom version of the movie *Baghdad Café* in 1990, Goldberg took on the genre again in 2003, with *Whoopi*. In it, her character, Mavis Rae, was a one-R&B-hit wonder who now runs a frowsy Manhattan hotel. But she was really just Whoopi makin'

Whoopee. She sets the tone of the series immediately in the pilot when, puffing on a cigarette behind the check-in desk, she's up-braided by a guest. "You know, secondhand smoke kills," he says. Whoopi snaps back, "So do I, baby—*walk on!*"

Goldberg told reporters that she wanted the show to be "kind of like Archie Bunker 2003," by which I don't think she meant she wants be perceived as a complacent bigot. Rather, I assume she intends to tell it like it is, honey. "People [in America] don't know the difference between Persians and Arabs," she tells the hotel handyman, Nasim (Omid Djalili), an Iran-bred Persian, "and frankly, they don't care."

Whoopi was created by *That '70s Show* executive producers Bonnie and Terry Turner. They and Goldberg think that educated black people using slang incorrectly is a stitch (lawyer Courtney threatens a tough black kid by saying that he'll "burst a cap up in here"), and they exploit the sad fact that audiences seem to love the spectacle of white people trying too hard to "be black." Goldberg positions her own character as a middle-aged fuddy-duddy—Mavis refers to "that hippety-hoppity music"—and her show came off both jaded and dated. It lasted a single season. Goldberg has settled for what she has for far too long: posing as an obstreperous rebel when she's really just a Hollywood square.

Love

The Best Episode of *The Twilight Zone*

"The Dummy"

Rod Serling was at his finest when he avoided his kneejerk tendency to write uplifting parables or condemnations against, oh, pretty much any of the seven deadly sins except adultery (ironic for a handsome married guy who worked himself to death at age fifty). His chief virtue as a writer—and a quality that helps a small percentage of his work stand out in our new century—was his interest in desperate, out-of-luck people, the shabby-genteel, fellows hard up for cash or trapped in crappy jobs they hated. Submitted for your perusal: "The Dummy." I know, Michael Redgrave had done this theme before and better in *Dead of Night* (1945), but Cliff Robertson's performance as a miserably sweaty ventriloquist whose life is taken over by his dummy is really terrific. Serling's teleplay captures a number of numbing show-biz cliches and gives them a renewed ability to make us squirm. Among these are the creepy nightclub owner who pressures Robertson to mingle with the paying customers in hopes of attracting more business, as contrasted to Robertson's character, a man who, pathetically but in a minor way heroically, perceives himself as an artist who shouldn't be put through such indignity. The final twist—ventriloquist and dummy swap bodies—is both predictable and undercut by the cheap-ass special effects the *Zone*'s budget was limited to. Serling's final voiceover send-off— "It's called the old switcheroo . . ."—is lame and eminently snip-worthy. Thanks to Robertson's vanity-free acting, "The Dummy" is unnerving in a way that too few *Twilight*s are, because we can identify with the ventriloquist's feelings of despair and contempt for the tyranny of lesser men who wield power over us.

Hate

The Two Worst Episodes of *The Twilight Zone*

"To Serve Man" and "Time Enough At Last"

Like P. G. Wodehouse and the films of David Fincher, *The Twilight Zone* is something best grown-out-of by the time you become an adult. Creator-writer-host Rod Serling himself seemed fixated on another adolescent pleasure: the surprise-twist endings of short stories by the likes of O. Henry and Saki, mistaking them for profound ironies. A New York teleplay writer who saw the "Golden Age of Television" melting fast, Serling hied off to the West Coast to spend much of the rest of his career writing Hollywood-liberal parables of tolerance, coming out strongly against greed and vanity, and in favor of the downtrodden, the Little Man, except when "little" was literal. In "The Last Night of a Jockey," Mickey Rooney was a petulant horse-monkey who wanted to become tall, and for his hubris started denting the ceiling with a painful growth spurt. As usual, the message was a tidy cliché: Be careful what you wish for.

Probably Serling's most famous *Zone* teleplay is "To Serve Man," the final-scene of which is a cornball-joke punchline. Aliens—called Kanamits—arrive on Earth and they start arranging visits to their planets for humans. The head alien is always toting around a book, and some government types latch onto it, translating its title as "To Serve Man"—a peace tract. We see streams of people climbing into spaceships to be transported to, I dunno, Kanamitron, or Kanamitville months later. The alien-language code is broken and the government reps discover that the tome is . . . a cookbook! Too late! Thousands of humans die! "From dust to dessert," says Serling in one of his typically teeth-clenched little envois. Adapted from a story by respected sci-fi writer Damon Knight, which just goes to show how little you have to come up with to be respected in *that* field, "To Serve Man" is commonly cited among Zonies as a fave-rave.

The other episode every fan seems to go ga-ga over is "Time Enough at Last." In the future, Burgess Meredith, a compulsive reader, becomes the last man on Earth after what seems a nuclear catastrophe. Note to self: Rod Serling came out against nukes and war! A solitary type, Meredith is delighted. He picks through the rubble, finding whole libraries. "Time enough at last!" he exclaims. To read forever; he'll finally get around to finishing, oh, I don't know, probably *Studs Lonigan*. As he bends over to pick up a book, his glasses fall off and break. Boo-hoo. I watched this episode with my youngest daughter and she immediately said, "Why doesn't he just look around among the dead people until he finds glasses close to his prescription?" Tell it to the Zonies, Laura . . .

Love

Twin Peaks's Pilot Episode: The Deflowering of TV's Narrative Innocence

Twin Peaks (1990–1991) was that rarity: a piece of avant-garde pop art that attracted a mass audience. In fact, a sure sign of its popularity is that its innovations were quickly absorbed into the culture, becoming commonplaces, and then banalities. As I write, you never hear anyone talk about the greatness of *Twin Peaks* or its novel oddity: evidence that it aired at all, that it pulled in what would now, in the cable-TV era, be a blockbuster "33 share," that is, a third of all televisions in America were tuned in to its premiere. The show is consigned mostly to TV history books, or the occasional appearance of one of its actors, to which the series is affixed as a credit. When Kyle MacLachlan had a run on *Sex and the City*, he was most frequently cited as "*Twin Peaks*'s Kyle MacLachlan"; *Peaks* pop up whenever Russ Tamblyn (once upon a time *The Boy with the Green Hair*, now known mostly as father of God-talking *Joan of Arcadia* star Amber Tamblyn, and *Peaks*'s much-needed but unreliable psychiatrist Dr. Jacoby) still gets work. The only performer who shook off the *Twin Peaks* label quickly was Lara Flynn Boyle, and that required not only joining *The Practice* but dating Jack Nicholson and turning herself into a party-girl toothpick—tough work for one gal, no matter how tough she's proven to be.

When it premiered, *Twin Peaks* was hot stuff because feature-film director David Lynch was deigning to work in the TV medium. Do-

ing so just four years after the haunting yet crowd-pleasing nightmare that was *Blue Velvet*, this was news. Most movie directors, it
was then thought, waited until their careers were washed up before
doing television. TV critics, unused to rich, creamy surrealism after a
steady diet of starched irony, burped all over themselves trying to
come up with clever ways to describe what had washed up onto the
shores of their living rooms with the cold, blue corpse of Laura
Palmer. I went with "*Mayberry RFD* goes *Psycho*" and "*Pee wee's
Playhouse* has a nervous breakdown," and I'm here to tell you I'm
properly abashed.

Looking back—and you can bet *Peaks*, which inspired everything
from a fan magazine, *Wrapped In Plastic*, to the short-lived Warner
Bros. Records contract of soundtrack singer Julie Cruise, is probably
not a big seller on tape or DVD on Amazon.com these days, so few
people *are* looking back—the series was most valuable for the way it
played with TV-time and narrative conventions. The press and the
show's insta-fans seized on Lynch's cutest conceits—the way
MacLachlan's FBI agent Cooper repeatedly savored "hot black coffee
and cherry pie"; the way a catatonic woman who carried a log
around was called The Log Lady. It was, however, *Peaks*'s storytelling that remains distinctive, and rarely copied. (The 1993 Oliver
Stone–Bruce Wagner foolishness *Wild Palms* is the most notable,
misbegotten exception that proves the rule.)

Lynch was able to approximate the pace and heavy drift of our
dream lives and deployed this technique in the service of a conventional murder mystery. "Who killed Laura Palmer?" the ads read, a
mantra repeated in the show and all over America for a few months.
The revelation of Laura's murderer—her father Leland, possessed, I
believe, by a psychotic soul referred to as "Killer Bob"—could never

live up to the national hype. Lynch was freed to pursue even more outre-for-prime-time visual strategies including a dancing dwarf, blood-red curtains, and a conflagration that portended Lynch's underrated 1992 feature-film extension of the franchise, *Twin Peaks: Fire Walk With Me.* Without the mystery-framework, however, the TV show's ratings plunged.

Nonetheless, Lynch had deflowered the American television audience, snatched away the lulling comfort we'd felt for decades that, whenever we turned on the tube, we could apply a form, or a format, to what we saw. If network television could be so easily undone, or underdone, or half-baked, or overcooked—take one movie director, add a TV writer-producer (Mark Frost: *Hill Street Blues*), and call me with the Nielsens in the morning—then we could take nothing for granted from this point on. It was only a matter of time until the Beckett-like absurdism of the final episode of *Seinfeld*, '80s-babies-nostalgia for narrative-imploding dreck like *Saved by the Bell* (enshrined by fake-hipster dreck-boosters like the writer Chuck Klosterman) and—a far more banal yet "real" nightmare of prime time; the *truly* bad version of *Fire Walk With Me*—NBC's maggot-feast, *Fear Factor.*

Hate

Final Episodes

Remember the group hug that concluded *The Mary Tyler Moore Show?* When Lou Grant uttered an utterly uncharacteristic line—"I treasure you people"—and then the medium's preeminent "workplace family" grouped, groped, and grokked each other, even moving over, as one waddling group, to get a box of tissues? 'Twas mildly funny—not really up to that great show's standards.

Remember the final shot of *M*A*S*H*? Alan Alda's Hawkeye—who'd slowly but surely become the show's portentous if martini-swilling voice of God, passing judgment upon all—looked down from the helicopter winging him away from Korea to . . . where? The Playboy Mansion? Heaven? Only then he looked down to see that his pal B. J. had formed the word "Goodbye" in rocks for Hawkeye's aerial pleasure and final ego-stroke? Ghastly! *So* atypical of the series' ostentatious surface cynicism, *so* typical of that series' underlying sentimentality and its steady erosion into wiseguy-worship.

In general, it's very tough to wrap up a series, especially one that develops a loyal, affectionate following. Most shows do it unmemorably: Do you recall the final episodes of *All in the Family, Dallas*, or *Melrose Place*? No reason to—nothing memorable about them. In the case of *All in the Family*, all that was happening was that widower Archie was being manipulated by the man who inhabited him, Carroll O'Conner, into suffering through a new, far more banal show, *Archie's Place*. For serialized shows that attract fans intensely committed to characters and plot-lines (think *X-Files*; think *Buffy the Vampire Slayer*) the most the creators can do is try to wrap up ongoing stories and send characters off with a certain clear-eyed finality that leaves viewers misty-eyed and satisfied.

In rare cases, a series built to an inevitable climax: The classic example is *The Fugitive*, until *M*A*S*H*'s farewell the highest-rated final episode ever. In 1967, nearly 46 million people tuned in to see whether David Janssen's Dr. Richard Kimble would finally corner his ultimate quarry, the one-armed man. Innocent times, those:

Does anyone doubt that, if done today—and they *tried* to do it, bringing back *The Fugitive* with *Wings*'s Tim Daly in the title role, fleetingly, in 2001—that Kimble would *not* catch the single-limbed villain?

In other cases, particularly ensemble comedies, it's extremely difficult to give the audience its emotional release and still conclude with a funny finale. Here, *Seinfeld* is distinctive. Its 1998 send-off was apparently intentionally unfunny, as though Jerry Seinfeld and cocreator Larry David had so overthought the concept of the last episode, were so committed to doing a sitcom in a way no one else had done it before, that they lost touch with everything people liked about the show (i.e., its four core characters) and wrote it as a Beckett play, with the *Seinfeld* cast trapped in a prison both real and metaphorical: the penitentiary of success. Not a wet eye across America and nary a chuckle either.

At the other extreme, there's the 2004 so-long-it's-been-good-to-know-ya episode of *Sex and the City*. This one was weighed down with cultural baggage: Could these women who'd spent seven years being pals to each other, independent of the men that came in and out of their lives, just be sent off to continue their pal-ship into eternity or late-middle-age, whichever came first? Of course not, and so star and executive producer Sarah Jessica Parker rewarded herself by bagging The One That Always Got Away, Chris Noth's Mr. Big, who in the final seconds suddenly accrued a "real" name: John. It was the punchline to a typically randy *Sex* joke—"Big John"! But the show seemed to punish the other characters: Cynthia Nixon, whose Miranda, a Manhattan lawyer who avoided becoming a shark, was always the most independent and feisty and successful of the quartet. She was consigned to a hellish existence in Brooklyn, living with hubby, baby, and a stroke-victim mother-in-law. Kim Cattrall's screw-crazy, screw-loose Samantha, finally given some humanity by giving her breast cancer (think about *that* cruelty for a moment), rated nothing more than one more nude-scene orgasm as her final shot at TV immortality. Humiliatin'!

Some series had startling conclusions that read better than they played. *St. Elsewhere*'s entire run was apparently the dream of an autistic child. As a narrative solution, it was like a bad Ray Bradbury short story. But one show dreamt, startled, *and* amused. I speak, of course, of the brilliant ending of a not-especially-brilliant series, *Newhart*, the 1982–1990 Bob vehicle in which he was Dick Loudon, a Vermont inn owner. The show was affable enough, but its only genius stroke in eight years came in its final seconds, when Bob's Dick, conked out by an errant golf ball, woke up in bed—and not with the wife played in *Newhart* by bland Mary Frann, but next to the older *Bob Newhart Show*'s glammy, gravel-voiced Suzanne Pleshette. He was Dr. Bob Hartley and she was Emily again and the entire *Newhart* series had been a dream conjured by the marvelous psychologist of that infinitely superior 1972–1978 sitcom. The moment dissolved the show you were watching—as pure an example of deconstruction as any media theorist could devise. And damn funny.

Love

TV Math: John Travolta + Gabe Kaplan × *Happy Days* −
Saved by the Bell = *Welcome Back, Kotter*

When *Welcome Back, Kotter* premiered in 1975, it wasn't a star vehicle for John Travolta—it was a video platform for the hot, youngish comic who played the teacher, Gabe Kaplan. One of the first to start the trend for stand-ups leaving nightclubs for the far more lucrative world of sitcoms; in a sense, we have him to thank for Roseanne, Tim Allen, and, lord-a-mercy, Brett Butler. Kaplan had been a smooth stage performer, but throughout Kotter's four-season stint, his primary facial expression was a fixed smirk, and he was as stiff as the bristly mustache that almost hid that smirk. Lest we forget where he'd come from, the producers had Kaplan doing bits from his stand-up act in nearly every episode, the material either awkwardly worked into the plot or used as stand-alone scenes to begin and end a half-hour. Watching him in reruns, Kaplan looks noticeably ill at ease. It's no wonder he opted out of television once the series left the air. A wise investor and a canny gambler, Kaplan is apparently doing fine, thank you.

The premise of *Kotter*—Brooklyn guy comes back to his 'hood to teach and encounters a new generation of hoodlums—served as a showcase for a motley quartet: Travolta as Vinnie Barbarino; Ron Palillo as whiny Arnold Horshack, the prototype for the grotesque Screech on the hideous *Saved by the Bell* fifteen years later; Lawrence-Hilton Jacobs as smoothie Freddie "Boom Boom" Washington and who went on to be a prolific TV director; and Robert Hegyes as dim-witted Juan Epstein. Collectively, this gang, the Sweathogs, were sort of The Marx Brothers do *West Side Story*. Indeed, Hegyes had Harpo's nimbus of hair and inflected his lines like Chico.

But the chief pleasure of watching *Kotter* now is what made the girls in the studio audience scream in the mid-'70s: Travolta. Sure, our good will toward Vinnie Barbarino these days is the kick we get knowing that this shaggy-haired kid would become a pop-culture icon in *Saturday Night Fever*, prove his legit acting chops in Brian DePalma's perennially underrated *Blow Out*, and embody the ultimate Sweathog nightmare in *Pulp Fiction*. There is no clue, though, that he will make *Battlefield Earth*.

Travolta steals every second of *Kotter*. His Brooklyn accent is more convincing than anyone else's in the cast, and, among his costars, he exudes a friendliness and vulnerability that makes the machine-gun pace of Kaplan's jokes bearable. In his time, Vinnie was Fonzie with soul; seen now, he's Travolta ascending the roller-coaster of his fame.

Hate

Chuck Barris: Confessions of a Crappy Mind

Hey, I like George Clooney a lot—*Out of Sight, O Brother Where Art Thou* (a thrillingly go-for-broke, underrated performance), *Ocean's Eleven*, and bully for him for being loyal to the flaky vision of his pal Steven Soderberg and trudging through *Solaris* like a trouper. But I can't subscribe to what amounts to his overseeing a cultural revisionism regarding Chuck Barris, the purveyor of game-show shit, enshrined as a misunderstood genius in Clooney's film adaptation of Barris's book *Confessions of a Dangerous Mind* (2002). I can see why a venturesome show-biz maverick like Clooney would be attracted to the idea that a venturesome show-biz maverick like Barris would write a pseudo-autobiography that made himself out to be a CIA assassin. A government tool instead of just a game-show tool. I can only hazard that to Clooney, all this appeals to an actor's sense of reinvention and the redemption of one's deepest, most neurotic self by making a pile of dough and then doing a disappearing act.

Clooney's an artist and I'm a critic, so it falls to me to point out that Barris is a pernicious fraud and a cynical putz-up of the culture who's not going to get his wish, to have it both ways: wealth *and* respect; fame *and* mysterioso obscurity. After starting out his career under the tutelage of a more polished, more assiduously conventional TV huckster, Dick Clark, Barris left ABC in 1965 with the idea for a syndicated show, *The Dating Game*. Three hidden-by-a-partition "eligible bachelors" answered often-smutty prewritten questions from a single young woman, after which she chose her date. That many of the contestants were professional actors or fledgling performers, for instance, a young, smart-enough-to-look-embarrassed Steve Martin, was not widely known.

The show, airing in the afternoon and providing its middle-class audience of work- and stay-at-homes with a whiff of the period's vaunted sexual revolution, was a smash, and Barris followed it up a year later in '66 with *The Newlywed Game*. In that show, freshly hitched couples had to guess each other's answers to often-smutty questions. Produced by his own company, the shows were sizzlers sufficient to be moved onto prime-time network TV—his old home,

ABC. After a few more copycats—these, however, duds like *How's Your Mother-In-Law?* and *The Family Game*—Barris came up with the most compleat embodiment of his own remark, quoted in Jefferson Graham's history of the game show, *Come On Down!!!*—"TV does not make meaningful statements." He birthed *The Gong Show* for NBC in our bicentennial year, 1976.

The Gong Show was a forerunner of reality TV: *Survivor* as a talent contest. Mostly fourth-rate celebrity judges such as Jaye P. Morgan, *M*A*S*H*'s Jamie Farr, "film critic" Rex Reed, and the actually-quite-a-stitch post-burlesque comic Rip Taylor watched intentionally bad performances by putative amateurs. As the show became a cool pop goof, there were occasional appearances by bigger names, like Paul Newman. (There were ringers—Paul Reubens, by then a veteran of the L.A. improv company The Groundlings, introduced Pee-wee Herman to television here.) When a judge could stand no more, he or she slammed a giant gong and the act was given the hook. A modern-day freak-show, *Gong* was hosted by Barris himself, whose mock-shy mannerisms—leering grin, hat pushed down over his eyes, twitchy, arhythmic clapping as he spoke—exerted their own odd pull on viewers. More a cultural phenomenon than his biggest hit (both *Dating* and *Newlywed Games* ran longer), *Gong* provoked snarls from media-watchdogs who thought it lowered lowbrow taste even further.

This missed the point. People have watched junk since TV began, knowing it's junk. Barris's contemptible smarm—his bottomless nihilism, judging everything from romance to marriage to talent as being void, a pathetic joke, a useless aspiration—is what makes the elevation of this smart, devious hack elevated to innovator status so meretricious. That, and the fact that he couldn't take the heat. In interview after interview given around the time of the Clooney-directed *Dangerous Mind* film, Barris claimed that he left the TV industry because he couldn't take "the criticism." Then, of course, he pulled the usual switcheroo executed by the whiney performers, by repeatedly saying that "TV criticism is pointless." No one calls Barris on the fact that his next and last game show, a bit of carny sexism called *The $1.98 Beauty Contest*, came and went in 1978 and exposed him as having used up his moment in the zeitgeist, thus hastening his departure from the scene.

Few people would ever want to sit through an entire rerun of *The Gong Show* now, even if its title has entered the language as a useful term for odious deceit: In December 2003, former Georgia senator Max Cleland condemned the Bush government's committee set up to investigate what the administration knew about the threat of terrorist attacks before 9/11 by saying "This investigation is . . . compromised. . . . This is *The Gong Show*; this isn't protection of national security."

Oh, yeah: Chuck Barris did one good creative thing in his life. No joke. He wrote Freddie Cannon's 1962 number-three hit "Palisades Park," an absolutely first-rate pop record. But as a contributor to entertainment, let alone society, Barris's rollercoaster ride after that went straight to hell.

Love

The Best Episode of the Best Family Show Ever:
"The Quilting" (1976) on *The Waltons*

This 1972–1981 series about life on the mountain, based on the autobiographical writings of Earl Hamner, Jr., who also served as the show's narrator, is lost in many people's memories as a sentimental, preachy show—*Big House on the Mountain*. The show's closing shot of the Walton house at night, as we hear voices— "Good night, Mama!" "Good night, John-Boy!"—led to countless cornpone parodies. Unlike the sanctimonious coat of lacquer Michael Landon applied to Laura Ingalls Wilder, Hamner, who helped produce the show, maintained a nicely crisp, dry tone to this family saga, especially in its early seasons. The show centered around Hamner's alter ego, the aspiring Thomas Wolfeian John-Boy, played by Richard Thomas with wet-eyed earnestness and a winning tendency to whip off his steel-rimmed glasses with one hand when he was done with what he considered a particularly felicitous piece of writing—journalism, a poem, a chapter in a novel, a journal entry. John-Boy's pride in his own work is one of the rare portrayals in any format of the secret pleasure writers take in savoring the completion of a piece of work.

In the episode I've singled out as the exemplar of everything good about *The Waltons*, the theme is all about letting people make their own decisions. The chief plot point turns around a quilting party to be held for eldest daughter Mary Ellen (Judy Norton-Taylor); her mother (tart Michael Learned) and grandmother (the so-tart-she-stings Ellen Corby) accept this tradition as part of life, since it serves as a "coming-out party" for the budding seventeen-year-old, the signal that boys can come a-courtin' for her. But Mary Ellen is intent on going to nursing school and leading an independent life; she wants no part of the quilting—a not-so-subtle metaphor for the fabric of family life—gets angry and runs away. Grandma and Mama Walton think Mary Ellen is just being teenage-typical stubborn, but the clan's wise father, John Walton, a wonderfully wuffly and wry Ralph Waite, takes the young woman's reservations seriously, and thinks Mary Ellen should decide for herself what she wants to do.

This was typical of the show, which prized individuality and personal dignity above all, even if it tested the messy interconnections of large-family life. The episode's subplot involved a contest Grandma enters to provide a slogan for a detergent's radio promotion. Unsure of her writing skills, she lets John-Boy write her entry. Without telling him, though, she ultimately enters her own prosaic prose, which wins the fifteen-dollar cash prize. Grandma's sense of ethics won't permit her to use someone else's words as her own. When Grandma wins, John-Boy graciously congratulates her.

If all this doesn't sound very dramatic, well, it is. Mary Ellen gets a fine, spitting speech about how she resents the quilting for the way it will "put me on the market for marriage . . . I am not a piece of merchandise!"

When a boy comes to woo Mary Ellen with flowers, Papa Walton warns him, "Mood she's in, you better be ready to duck." The boy says soberly, "Oh, I always am with Mary Ellen, sir."

"Uh-huh," says Papa dubiously, as though the kid is underestimating his daughter's wrath. Interestingly, it's John-Boy, who himself wants to leave the mountain to launch his own career, who argues with her that the quilting isn't a slave contract but "it's a gift . . . to remind you of people who were fond of you when you were growing up."

Still, Mary Ellen resists, leading to an exchange that also distinguishes *The Waltons* from most family shows of its, or any, era.

"She's got her feet dug in worser than a Missouri mule," Mama complains to Papa.

"Well," notes Papa, "she does live in a coop with three feisty hens."

"I am not a feisty hen!" says Mama indignantly.

"No?" says Papa, with a discreet, humorous leer. "You look pretty good to this old rooster."

Why, later you even see Mama and Papa snuggling in bed—no big deal; no rib-nudging or sniggering, just life as it's experienced among people at any age.

The Waltons costarred Will Geer, a folksinger who'd been blacklisted during the McCarthy era, as Grandpa. The series featured an underrated performance by Mary Elizabeth McDonough as the shiningly pretty second daughter, Erin. In later seasons, *The Waltons* suffered the usual strain of running out of plots and introducing too many characters, by marrying off most of the kids and hauling on a lot of wooden spouses. For most of its run, *The Waltons* achieved what it set out to do: make lyrically idealized a group of lives lived in splendid isolation, with the promise of escape to a bigger world for those who yearned for it.

Hate

Mr. Landon Builds His Dream *House*

Laura Ingalls Wilder wrote the autobiographical series of books chronicling her life in the late-nineteenth-century with an uncommon grace and simplicity that has intrigued, educated, and expanded the popular conceptions of the American Midwest for generations of young and adult readers. Michael Landon, having climbed down off the hobbled horse of an exhausted *Bonanza* in 1973, immediately traded in his Little Joe–the-young-son cowboy hat for a wider-brimmed husband-father-farmer's chapeau to star in, executive-produce, and frequently direct the Wilder stories. *Little House* was a network hit for eight years, made a star of future Actors Guild president Melissa Gilbert, who played a cherub-faced Laura, and paved the way for Landon's oily-slick *Highway to Heaven*.

Along the way, Landon's highjacking of the *Prairie* sentimentalized Wilder's spare realism, and beefed up the element of masculine discipline in Wilder's universe. The beloved star, who died in 1991, always had a warm, ready grin, but behind it was an egocentrism that imbued his Charles Ingalls with a stern, all-knowing wisdom that undermined the explicit details Wilder provided of women's strong-willed and strong-backed contributions to settling the land and raising families.

There's no reason a TV series should hew slavishly to its source material . . . unless the new interpolations are inferior to the material already at hand. In its early seasons, Landon was content to reproduce many of Wilder's semifictional narratives—he even did a reasonably good job of including biographical material about Wilder's family others had unearthed. But starting in 1977, when Victor French's Mr. Edwards—neighbor-farmer, family-friend—left the series, Landon turned *Little House* into a boardinghouse, and the muscular, curly-locked executive producer started marrying off his show's daughters to men foreign to Wilder's stories. He had his writers dream up increasingly far-fetched plots that had them moving around the country, giving birth, dealing with the loss of children and grandchildren. At least one blind character, not Melissa Sue Anderson's Mary, but her hubby, Adam, regained his sight, via—well, it was a miracle!

One of the best things that can be said of Landon's *Little House* is that it gave gainful employment for Linwood Boomer, who played Adam, and perhaps gave him the time and money to dream up the beguiling sitcom he subsequently created: *Malcolm in the Middle*.

Love

Batman: The Dark Knight Is an Asshole

With its stilted narration—"The Dynamic Duo is about to be perforated into human piano rolls!"—its comic-strip labelling of punches ("POW!" "BAM!"), and its capering Caped Crusader, the live-action TV version of the comic-book hero Batman set the entire comic-book industry back in such a way that it took literally decades to recover. (Yes, this is a "Love" entry; don't worry—I'll get there.) It required the iconoclastic work done near the end of the century in comics like Art Spiegelman's *Maus* and Alan Moore's auto-critique of the superhero format, *Watchmen*, to get comics thought of by the book-buying public as more than goofball camp, as irredeemable crap. The man who screwed up comics for thirty years or so was producer William Dozier.

Dozier's background lay in the flat middlebrow of '50s drama anthologies like *Playhouse 90* and *Climax* ("I had never read a Batman comic book [while growing up]," he sniffily said in Joel Eisner's *The Official Batman Batbook*, "I read *David Copperfield*, *Great Expectations*, things you were supposed to read"—hey, Bill: you could have read *both* kinds of lit, and Dickens was the serial-hero-spinner of his day anyway). But Dozier, an independent producer, was looking for a project to develop for the early-evening programming hours of ABC in 1964 when he learned of comic books' popularity among youngsters. He says he immediately read "seven or eight" copies of *Batman* and inspiration struck: "I had the simple idea of overdoing it, of making it so square and so serious that adults would find it amusing. I knew kids would go for the derring-do, but the trick would be to find adults who would either watch it with their kids, or to hell with the kids, watch it anyway."

Dozier cast Adam West as Batman after explaining to him that he had to play the role "as though we were dropping a bomb on Hiroshima, with that kind of deadly seriousness." It's a little-known fact that Dozier himself supplied the deep-voiced, mock-intense voiceover narration ("Meanwhile, at stately Wayne Mansion . . .") after discovering that the Screen Actors Guild, if he joined it, "has the best medical plan in the business."

Dozier surrounded unknowns West and Burt Ward's Robin with well-known midlevel performers as villains taken from the comic books, including impersonator Frank Gorshin as The Riddler in the 1964 premiere, and, over the years, Cesar Romero as The Joker, Burgess Meredith as The Penguin, and most famously, no fewer than three incarnations of Catwoman (Julie Newmar, Lee Meriweather, and Eartha Kitt). And then there were the non-comic-book creations, like an excruciatingly mugging Milton Berle as Louie the Lilac.

The series, arriving in the same year that Susan Sontag published her culture-transforming essay "Notes on 'Camp,' " was uncanny, fully formed Camp right from the start. The question of whether Adam West was in on the joke or was merely a wooden actor will forever remain moot. His ponderous line readings, Robin's ever-increasingly rococo use of the phrase "Holy something" to express dismay (my favorite is "Holy Grammar"—after Robin notices the howler the Joker commits in saying "He who laughs last laughs good"), and deliberately primitive shots of the Dynamic Duo climbing a building via the Bat-rope (the camera tilting to show that West and Ward were merely walking along a skyscraper-set turned flat on its side). Combined with the overacting of the guest stars, all of it tapped into precisely what Dozier wanted. Kids took the show at face value, adults watched to feel smugly superior to what quickly became a word-of-mouth hit, airing not once but twice a week, on Wednesdays and Thursdays, the better to introduce and resolve yet another parody: the cliffhanger. Viewers were urged to tune in the following night, "same Bat-time, same Bat-channel!"

Batman is not a series that holds up beyond the episodes in which Gorshin does amazingly elastic work with his jaw-splitting facial expressions (you can see where Jim Carrey got a lot of tips on how to play Ace Ventura and The Mask) and Eartha Kitt is hissing like a sexy snake—for pure African-American bombshell quality, she beats the hell out of ABC's blaxploitation rip-off, *Get Christie Love!* (1974–1975). But the series possesses an enviable go-for-broke energy that speaks well for its source material. It's taken me years to overcome my detestation of a series that ridiculed a form I've enjoyed in comic books and newspaper strips. One of the many small but satisfying pleasures of writing this book has been in re-viewing shows I thought I despised. I now acknowledge that the *Batman* TV show is actually—via that unpredictable combination of accident, greed, cynicism, good timing, and dumb luck that characterizes so many interesting pop phenomena—pretty damn funny. (And in an odd way, funny is what comic books and strips need more of now: as gorgeous as I think Chris Ware's *Jimmy Corrigan* books are and how stirringly emotional Michael Chabon's comics-soaked novel *The Adventures of Cavalier and Clay* is, the cultural shift has been to make the stuff solemn and arty, draining away much of the spirit of fun.)

Meanwhile, if the detritus of *Batman*—which burned out through overexposure after a mere two seasons—is the spate of memoirs by cast members (including Ward's truly icky tell-all about how much Bat-pussy he scored in his, er, prime), well, there's also the cultural corrective of designer/illustrator Chip Kidd's beautiful, mind-blowing 2001 book *Batman Collected*. It codifies the Camp, the sincerity, the artistry, the *fun* that is . . . Holy Batman!

Hate

Nostalgia as a Measure of Artistic Value

As a baby-boomer and a boy-man, I carry fond memories of old Westerns like Steve McQueen's *Wanted: Dead or Alive*—to have a sawed-off shotgun strapped to one's leg, what a cool way to deal with bullies! I watched everything Walt Disney put on the air in the mid- to late '60s, from *The Hardy Boys* to *Davy Crockett* to *Zorro*; my kid-libido was aroused by the mole on Anne Francis's cheek and her spike-heeled slither through *Honey West* (1965–1966).

I made a point of looking at these shows while researching this book, and I'm here to tell you: They're all crap. Oh sure, Steve Mc-Queen was pretty cool, but the plots of *Wanted* were wanting; the only Western I reevaluated that holds up as terse storytelling is *The Rifleman*, which was overseen in its early years by director Sam Peck-inpah. I had suspected that the nostalgia for the stuff I cherished as a youth wouldn't hold up to any adult measure of artistic quality, and man, was *that* right. Cable channels like Nickelodeon's prime-time Nick at Nite, TV Land, and GSN (formerly the Game Show Net-

work) have turned television's past into an ever-present. Because of
the reissue of many series on DVD, it seems as though all of television history now exists in the present. But this means that, now more
than ever, we need to remain unfogged by sentimentality to experience both enjoyment and whatever artistry TV has had to offer since
its birth. For too many viewers, old *and* young, nostalgia, affection
acquired during one's tender years, and quality intermingle. It's as
though the spiralling strand of critical evaluation is no longer a part
of millions of people's DNA.

Thus is garbage mulched in the damp mists of memory. Not just
The Red Skelton Show or *The Man From U.N.C.L.E.* or *The Brady
Bunch* but also idiotic time wasters like *The Dukes of Hazzard, The
Facts of Life,* and *CHiPs.* Partly this has to do with the Gen X phenomenon of TV-as-babysitter, As more parents were forced or chose
to enter the workforce, television became a source of comfort and
nurture as much as it was entertainment, which explains the intense
bond some feel toward crap like syndicated afternoon reruns of
Scooby Doo or *Punky Brewster.* Many of us no longer consider a
show such as *Melrose Place* and say, "Well, *there's* an interesting little
time capsule of clothing styles and melodrama-formula that worked
for a while." No; people claim to *love* the show, freezing a period in
our lives when we used to gather together to watch and hoot and
hiss and identify with or feel affection for the flimsy characters with
big emotions and bigger hairdos. At least one writer, Chuck
Klosterman, has made a minicareer out of such gleeful garbage-
picking; one of the longest chapters in his 2003 book *Sex, Drugs
and Cocoa Puffs* is devoted to a loving reverie about the worthless
Saturday afternoon sitcom *Saved by the Bell.* Klosterman makes a
fetish of worthlessness; he's one of those hollow hipsters for whom

cheesiness is a term of praise. For him and nostalgists like him, it's funny to enshrine crap TV as cool cultural metacritiques.

Add the elements of irony and retro-hipness to nostalgia, and it becomes a suffocating method of evaluating television's past. For Klosterman and his ilk, there are no standards; everyone's opinion is as valid as anyone else's; *Family Ties* is as good as *The Mary Tyler Moore Show*; *21 Jump Street* is as good as *The Sopranos*. Nostalgia is a narcotic from which we should all be weaned. It's called growing up; developing a sense of the world and the arts beyond TV references. I really like the formal rigor of *Perry Mason* reruns, but I also know that that same quality is in more subtle abundance in an Anthony Hecht poem. I like Claire Danes's acting, too, but I hope you're not going to tell me you think *My So-Called Life* is as good as Jane Austen . . .

Love

Pamela Anderson's Breasts

Constrained by their owner's "Tool Time Gal" outfit when she was the Dagmar of *Home Improvement*, Pamela Anderson's breasts first surfaced when she joined the lifeguard saga *Baywatch* in 1990. As the terribly earnest, perpetually frowning lifeguard C. J. Parker, Anderson strode across the sand looking as if the heads of newborn twins were just breaking the surface of her red bathing suit. Surely, this was the happiest one-piece in the universe.

After that, it was a series of ups and downs for Anderson's best-known glands. There were the numerous talk-show appearances in which Jay or Conan "fumbled" to attach a microphone wire to a tenuous bit of fabric that might at any moment release the golden globes, proof of the principle of Willing Disbelief. Viewers never questioned this gambit, but was any other celebrity not miked *before* coming onstage? This was a gag as old as—well, as old as Charo.

Then there was the infamous home movie during which Anderson's pair played volleyball while husband Tommy Lee's baseball-batlike penis took up more home-movie camera time, and only a churl would deny the wooden fellow his moment of glory. The illicit private tape and Anderson's peeled-grape spreads for *Playboy* lacked the satisfaction of TV-sex—the feeling one gets that you are glimpsing things you ought not to be seeing on this mass medium, on the small screen that tries so vainly to be clean and moral and, therefore, radiating all the more erotic allure when a happy hussy like Anderson bursts forth to tease us. This is the pleasure of sexual shapes and suggestivenesses framed on the small, noncable screen—the last pop-culture bastion of naughtiness, shame, and lust about to bust.

There was a worrisome period circa Anderson's syndicated adventure-spoof *V.I.P.*, in which her gals were said to have been reduced via surgical procedure, but as the years go by, the breasts seem to have regained their hard, round prominence. Long may the doughty troupers rise to her occasion.

Hate

Sex on Network TV: Just Say No

On sitcoms, it is always sought-after, talked about in cutesy euphemisms ("boinking"), and rarely achieved. In dramas, it tends to be abundant though largely unseen, a quick act of tension-release, a signal to the audience that it is watching either a "serious" show or a nighttime soap grope. No one fucks on network television; they make love, grab a quickie, nurse their blue balls. The older television gets, the less sexy network TV becomes, even as the medium makes periodic announcements of new boldness (bare asses will be seen tonight on *NYPD Blue*—parental discretion advised!) from which it then retreats, petrified of sponsors withdrawals, congressional hearings, scoldings in the press.

The pleading for sex from a spouse in shows like *Everybody Loves Raymond, Friends, According to Jim*, and countless others is seedy and often creepy. Jim Belushi is kidded for having a "small penis." An entire episode of *King of Queens* revolves around costar Leah Rimini's breasts being fondled by her boss's four year-old son and the ethical/class/taste dilemmas that raises (the episode is entitled "Mammary Lane.") In *Friends*, Chandler doesn't want to have sex in front of Ross and Rachel's baby, with whom Chandler and Monica have been entrusted for a few hours. Chandler whines, "I can't say 'hump' or 'screw' in front of the b-a-b-y." He gets big laughs for spelling out "baby" but saying "hump" and "screw." This is depressing.

Only one show has made sex look like the fun, dangerous, fraught, wild act it can be: *Buffy the Vampire Slayer*, whether it was Buffy and Angel screwing until their here-today, gone-tomorrow souls united, or Buffy giving the sneering Johnny-Rotten-mode vampire Spike a mercy fuck, or Willow and Tara slurping and caressing in the most dizzyingly ecstatic depiction of lesbian ardor any network has let slip past its censors. How? "It's a fantasy show," creator Joss Whedon has said impishly, understanding how important genre distinctions are to networks and how irrelevant they are to viewers. "We can get away with a lot more than a conventional drama."

In TV history, there was more sex in the twitch in Elizabeth Montgomery's *Bewitched* nose, in the ritual unveiling of Heather Locklear's legs in a *Melrose Place* skirt, in the unpeeling of George Clooney's *ER* green scrubs than there has been in all the "frank" sex-talk and sex-organ-outline glimpses on modern sitcoms and dramas. Even a figure as jaded as Howard Stern has said, "I learned everything I know about sex from TV." His example was Tina Louise's Ginger on *Gilligan's Island*. On network television, it is the repressed stuff, the suggestion of lewdness, the glimpse of curve and muscle beneath strained garments—not the talk and the wink and the rare full-on sighting of tit or ass—that gives TV its greatest erotic charge. The medium is a force field of sexual power and energy. Too bad it is so rarely harnessed for its true potency.